ESSENTIALS OF

Operational Research
and its Management Applications

R. S. Stainton

B.A., M.Tech., Ph.D., F.B.C.S., F.I.M.A., F.O.R.,
The Henley Administrative Staff College

MACDONALD AND EVANS

MACDONALD & EVANS LTD.
Estover, Plymouth PL6 7PZ

First published 1977

ISBN: 0 7121 1522 6

MACDONALD AND EVANS LIMITED
1977

Printed in Great Britain by
Clarke Doble and Brendon Ltd., London & Plymouth

General Editor's Foreword

Books in the Essentials of Management series are designed for the executive director, manager, accountant, company secretary, administrator; in fact, anyone who is concerned with improving business efficiency.

Inevitably these "professionals" are busy men or women with limited free time at their disposal. Yet they must understand the latest techniques, principles, practices and developments to enable them to apply appropriate skills to the problems that arise.

In designing the books in this series we have concentrated on presenting the facts in an interesting and stimulating way, combining principles and practice. Case studies are integrated into the text, showing the real problems which may arise in the world of industry or commerce.

General Editor

Preface

Operational Research was first established during the Second World War of 1939–45. Before that time, managers were naturally looking for ways in which they could improve their own and their company's efficiency, but not in any formalised way. It was realised during the war, however, that better results would be obtained if experience and skills could be pooled and problems tackled in a scientific manner.

Since 1945, the effort in Operational Research has been applied to solving the problems in business, industry and government. The applications have been many and diverse, but to some extent they can be grouped together and represented by particular techniques or methodology.

It is the purpose of this book to discuss these techniques, and to show how they might benefit company operations. It should be borne in mind, however, that it has not been possible to identify all possible applications, only to highlight some by example. The reader who thinks about the techniques within the context of his own environment will gain the greatest advantage.

This book is intended as an introductory text. I am indebted to the many managers from industry and to the Operational Research specialists who have influenced directly or indirectly what I have written. This book will be of greatest interest to those who wish to obtain a broad view of Operational Research in a limited time. It will appeal to the manager and to the student alike.

1977   R.S.S.

Contents

CONTENTS

CHAPTER I

Background to Operational Research

THE DEFINITION OF O.R.

To provide an acceptable definition for Operational Research is probably ,the most difficult task in the whole of this book. For several years now Operational Research practitioners have argued amongst themselves about the precise nature of their job. They are yet to arrive at a consensus of opinion upon which they all agree, or even one which a majority might accept. Nevertheless the Operational Research Society does provide a somewhat lengthy definition which is reproduced below.

"Operational Research is the application of the methods of science to complex problems arising in the direction and management of large systems of men, machines, materials and money in industry, business, government, and defence. The distinctive approach is to develop a scientific model of the system, incorporating measurements of factors such as chance and risk, with which to predict and compare the outcomes of alternative decisions, strategies or controls. The purpose is to help management determine its policy and actions scientifically."

Despite this definition, the O.R. Society has recently undertaken a search for a more satisfactory definition, inviting each member to put forward other proposals. It will probably not be for some time, however, before a change will be made.

The reason for the difficulty in providing an effective

definition of O.R. lies in the nature of the subject itself. To elaborate on this statement at this stage would launch us immediately into our own attempts to define Operational Research which would clearly be inappropriate. We shall instead discuss the manner in which O.R. has developed over the years and the position it has now reached in both academic and industrial society.

THE BEGINNINGS OF O.R.

Like any branch of science, it could be said that its beginnings were when man first began to think about his environment. Once he had mastered rudimentary mathematics he set out to apply his newly-gained logical skills. He could look at ways in which he might improve the manner in which he worked and lived, and strive for greater efficiency by planning in advance what he hoped to achieve and how he should set about actually achieving it.

We might take any stage in history to illustrate this point, but perhaps an appropriate one might be the building of the pyramids during Egyptian times. It was well known that a three-four-five triangle would always contain a right angle between its two shortest sides (later to be proved conclusively by Pythagoras) and this fact was put to good use to ensure that the planes of the pyramids were truly set at right angles, as was necessary.

It might be conceivable to claim this innovation and application of a scientific principle as one of the first achievements of Operational Research. After all, the operation of building had been made much easier by the research into the manner in which the pyramid was to be built. Nevertheless, there would be some who would argue that it was a clear case of Work Study, and others who would say that it was simply Applied Mathematics.

Another name for Operational Research is Management Science, and for his work in improving the efficiency of companies in the early years of the twentieth century, F. W. Taylor is recognised as the father of Management Science. Yet Taylor is also considered to be the founder of Work Study. It is evident, therefore, that Operational Research has sprung from Work Study and from Applied Mathematics and, like every new branch of science, it is difficult to say precisely where one subject ends and the other begins.

OPERATIONAL RESEARCH AND WORLD WAR II

Operational Research really came to the fore and became established as a subject in its own right during World War II. It was essential at that time to deploy resources in the most economical and efficient ways. To ensure that this was done, a team of scientists was drawn together and instructed that they find solutions to pressing operational problems.

One in particular concerned the passage of merchant shipping from the United States to Great Britain. It provided an essential life-line for the survival of the country, yet German U-boats were causing havoc by sinking considerable numbers of ships in mid-Atlantic. The conclusion reached by the investigating team was that the merchant ships should sail in larger convoys, not singly as had once been thought to be the safest way. A convoy of ships could, of course, be destroyed in one grand strike, but provided security was sufficiently rigid, in the wide Atlantic a single convoy would be harder to find and that much easier to protect by combined Naval and Air forces. In contrast, smaller groups would enjoy scant protection and by combing the seas suitably well, the German Navy could pick off individual ships at will.

Many kinds of problems were tackled by the newly formed and mushrooming groups of Operational Research scientists, and like many other kinds of research activities in times of war, discoveries were made which have benefited mankind in peace time as well. World War II provided the foundation for much of Operational Research as we know it today.

DEVELOPMENT SINCE WORLD WAR II

It was soon realised that the talents and experience of the wartime O.R. practitioners could be put to good use in the country's resurgent industries. In 1947 the Operational Research Society was formed and now membership of the Society has increased to over 3,000. All large companies boast an Operational Research department and there are few medium-sized companies who do not employ at least one practitioner. There is also a considerable number of consultancy companies specialising in Operational Research.

Professor Pat Rivett was appointed to the first chair in Operational Research at the University of Lancaster in 1961. He was previously head of Operational Research at the National Coal Board. It is now unusual not to find a professor in Operational Research at a British university, or at any university in the world for that matter.

The ways in which Operational Research have developed are diverse. It will be the purpose of this book to explain in later chapters how, and in what directions, Operational Research has developed since the early days and World War II.

RELATIONSHIP WITH OTHER SUBJECTS

The implication from the present definition of Operational Research provided by the Operational Research Society is that O.R. is inherently mathematical. It is for this reason that a new definition is currently being debated. It is fully recognised by O.R. practitioners that business activity is not as deterministic as they would perhaps like it to be. Many of the research findings of the behavioural sciences impinge upon Operational Research work, and without the full co-operation of, for example, the accountant in providing necessary data, the Operational Research scientist would find considerable difficulty in carrying out his task of providing optimum solutions. Not only does he need to co-operate with the behavioural scientist, the accountant, the economist, the psychologist, the cybernetician, and others, he needs to have a proper understanding of the work they do and how they do it.

A university course in Operational Research will embrace each of these subjects. It will also provide a comprehensive background in data processing, work study, organisation and methods, and the whole sphere of industrial engineering. The universities, and perhaps more particularly so the polytechnics, are conscious of the need for practical experience and, unlike many other academic subjects, a great deal of the graduate's time is spent on case studies and work on real-life problems in the business environment. In the world of Operational Research experience is equally as important as theory.

DISCUSSION QUESTIONS

1. What is the purpose of Operational Research?

2. Why is Operational Research called by that name?

3. When was Operational Research first applied?

4. In what associated subjects must an O.R. scientist develop his skills?

CHAPTER II

The Organisation and Effectiveness of Operational Research

THE REPORTING STRUCTURE

Most large companies nowadays have at least one member of staff whom they would classify as an Operational Research specialist. Several companies have large groups of such people, grouped into a recognisable departmental structure. Usually the Operation Research department reports to the Management Services Manager, who in turn reports to the Financial Director of the company. The sphere of responsibility of the Management Services Manager often extends to control of the Data Processing department (including programming, systems design and data preparation), Organisation and Methods, Work Study, and other like functions. Figure 1 illustrates a typical reporting structure chart.

Although it is common for Operational Research to report into Finance, it is by no means certain in all companies that this will be so. It is perhaps traditional that Finance should have control of Data Processing and consequently Operational Research, since in the first place it was Finance who produced the accounts, provided financial analysis, and were the keepers of the company's basic information store. The first applications of the computer were on behalf of Finance, and Operational Research specialists are frequently classified, not necessarily correctly, as people who are similar in the work they do to those who are in Data Processing.

If Operational Research, within the Management Services function, does not report into Finance, it is not so easy to say precisely where else it should report. If all or most of O.R. work within a company is concentrated in one particular area, say Production, then perhaps it makes sense for the O.R. department to be an integral part of Production.

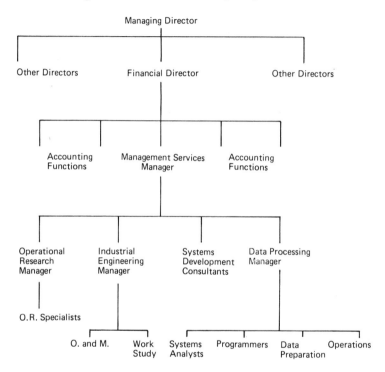

Fig. 1. A reporting structure chart

An example of dedication of this kind could be Work Study, who might see scope for their work in areas other than Production, but whose major task tends to be in the Production field and who therefore report through to the Production Director. Nevertheless, once a service department such as Operational Research is under the control of one particular function within the company, it must guard against becoming so immersed in that function's objectives that it sees those objectives as the ones for the company as a whole. Operational Research must maintain independence and not be under the influence of any single part of the company.

THE FUNCTION OF O.R.

The function of O.R. is to assist management in improving company efficiency and hence profitability in whatever way it possibly can. Increasing profit is synonymous with reducing cost, and so often the O.R. scientist is called in to determine ways of cutting costs.

Very often, one part of the company might see ways in which it can perform its tasks better and at lower cost, but unfortunately to the detriment of another part of the company. If the gain from making the changes in the first part is greater than the loss suffered by the second part then clearly making the change is worthwhile. An example might be the consideration of production run length in a batch processing company; a long run means fewer change-overs and therefore lower production costs, but the resulting high stocks may be inconvenient for Distribution to handle and cause them unnecessary additional costs in the form of transport charges and larger capacity warehouses. Thus, the role of the O.R. specialist is to steer a middle course through possibly opposing objectives within the company, so that ultimately the company as a whole is able to choose its best options.

For this reason, the O.R. department must be unbiased and be seen to lean only towards ways of improving company performance and effectiveness. This is no mean task and inevitably attitudes of mind and personalities will play their part. The O.R. scientist is trained to remain impartial and to approach the problems with which he is confronted in a clinical fashion.

MANAGEMENT RESPONSIBILITIES

It would be quite impossible for the O.R. practitioner to

even begin to carry out his work if he were not to receive the full support of all levels of management within the company. Yet, equally, it would be unrealistic to assume that he would in all circumstances receive such co-operation. Inevitably, occasions will arise when he will see the strength of one particular argument against another and will provide evidence in support of that particular argument.

Management responsibility rests in ensuring that the O.R. scientist has full support and a thorough and clear exposition of what the problem is and what achievement in the way of solution is expected of him. It must be agreed between both parties at what stage an acceptable solution has been reached and the "rules of the game" must not change whilst the investigation is being conducted and whilst the solution is being evolved. It will be necessary at times, of course, to take account of changing circumstances, but management must do all in their power to foresee possible changes and include them in the specification of the problem which they compile in the first place.

Company problems which can benefit from Operational Research treatment may be identified either by management themselves or by an astute Operational Research worker. It is usual for the more successful O.R. jobs to arise through an awareness on the part of the manager himself who is suffering the problem that O.R. analysis can help. The greater knowledge a manager has of Operational Research capabilities, the better able is the O.R. scientist to assist him. If the O.R. man is the first to identify a problem, he then has a selling job to do to convince the management involved that (a) they have a problem and (b) he can solve it. It is therefore a management responsibility to keep an open mind about the ways that service operations can help.

It is tempting for the O.R. scientist to accept an O.R. assignment which is ill defined. In many ways it gives him broader scope for his talents and he is not constrained to explore just one avenue of likely problems. Equally, it is far easier for company management to paint a general picture of their activity without properly defining what it is that troubles them most and then simply to ask the O.R. man to "do something about it". Seldom in such circumstances does either party achieve any satisfaction since the one has not truly said what he wants and the other has no real idea of what his mission is.

PERFORMANCE CRITERIA

The only way in which management and O.R. specialists can be sure that they are each pulling in the same direction is for them to acknowledge mutually agreed performance criteria. Usually, it is a difficult task to say precisely what it is that it is hoped to be achieved at the end of a study; the following example may serve to illustrate the point.

One particular company received complaints from its employees that the lifts serving the building in which they worked were functioning too slowly. The report from the lift manufacturer confirmed that it was not possible to make the lifts work any faster. They also expressed surprise at the complaint because no other company seemed to be suffering the same kind of problem. An O.R. group were commissioned to investigate the complaints and soon determined that within this particular company there appeared to be a greater necessity for personal message-carrying than in most other companies and that in the main these tasks were performed by the female clerical staff. They therefore resolved to see if there were any means by which the number of messages could be reduced, but in the meantime hit upon the idea that mirrors should be hung on the walls in the corridors where the lifts operated so that the young ladies might see themselves whilst they were waiting. As a direct result of installing the mirrors, the frequency of complaint diminished dramatically. Since the objective of the exercise was to achieve greater employee satisfaction, it could be argued that installation of the mirrors had achieved this, but it would be difficult to say precisely how well it had been achieved.

In most O.R. studies some measure of performance exists and may be determined in advance. Greater profit is obviously the ultimate performance criterion, but it is not always possible to say when greater profit has been obtained. Many O.R. studies rely upon intangible benefits, like those described above in satisfying the vanity of the young lady employees, to justify their implementation. When we consider Operational Research methods in greater detail in later chapters, we shall see how well-defined criteria of performance can be set.

OPERATIONAL RESEARCH TECHNIQUES

Operational Research relies upon scientific methodology to solve business problems. When using a mathematical analysis, it defines the problem in as precise a way as possible, representing the various aspects of the problem as mathematical relationships, or equations, which are known as "constraints". There must always be an end product to an Operational Research analysis and what it is hoped to be achieved must also be capable of being written down in mathematical form, as a mathematical equation. The objective is always to optimise that "end product", i.e. either to maximise or minimise, depending upon the requirements of the problem. The particular O.R. technique which is employed is the one which achieves the optimisation in the most effective way.

We see therefore that if a problem is to be tackled in a mathematically-based Operational Research way, it must firstly be reduced to mathematical equations which represent the way in which the company is run. These company rules or "procedures" are the constraints of the problem. It must also be possible to write the solution objectives in mathematical form, and this is known as the "objective function". The procedure is then to optimise the objective function within the stated constraints.

DISCUSSION QUESTIONS

1. Why is it commonly found that the Operational Research department reports to the Finance function?

2. How should the O.R. scientist approach the company problems with which he is faced?

3. Whose responsibility is it to identify the problems in the first place?

4. How does the O.R. scientist and the management for whom he is working know when he has completed a job satisfactorily?

5. What is the basic structure of an O.R. task?

CHAPTER III

Statistics - the Theory

FACTS FROM DATA

It is common in many companies to refer to tabulated
data which is compiled for management use as statistics.
However, the branch of mathematics known as Statistics
treats numerical data in a far more rigorous fashion and is
concerned with the measure of the probability of certain
facts being true, as well as their presentation. It is this
kind of statistics which enables management to take
decisions with a degree of confidence, with some knowledge of whether the data upon which they have taken
their decisions is representative or not.

It is not always convenient to treat all data in this
clinical way and often statistics in the sense of simple
tabulated data is accepted by management as an exact
representation of the facts. In the mind of the manager it
takes on the role of mathematical statistics, and decisions
are based on it which, given more detailed analysis, would
otherwise be suspect. The mathematician and the O.R.
man, however, consider statistics to be a shorthand way of
presenting results, providing few figures instead of many,
the few representing and illustrating the many.

Statistics is important in Operational Research because
it provides, in the mathematical sense, concise data upon
which O.R. studies may be based. As an example, if we
were examining the traffic intensity on a particular road
we should be more confused with the knowledge of all
vehicular movement on that road than we would with
hourly or daily figures. We would suffer mental indiges-

tion with all the data and would probably "not see the wood for the trees" as a result. We are content with the manageable data, but recognise that we may be ignoring other data of importance.

The Average

The simplest statistic in a mathematical sense is the average. Instead of placing on view all possible numbers in the set, we can describe them all by adding them together and then dividing by the number of separate entries we have in the set. The average so formed is suitably representative of all the numbers. Or is it?

Let us suppose that there are ten people standing outside the door and we are told that their average height is 1.75 metres. As a result, we might reasonably conclude that there are some slightly smaller than 1.75 metres and some slightly taller. Further perhaps it would not be unreasonable to assume five smaller and five taller. In making such assumptions we would be using more inform-ation than we had strictly been given; we know from common experience that people are about 1.75 metres in height, but it is unusual for them to vary greatly about that height, and that the ten people under consideration have most likely been chosen at random from people around us.

If we were to invite the ten people into the room, we would probably be surprised if we found that the group consisted of five giants and five midgets. We would be equally surprised if nine of them were each 1.50 metres tall and the tenth 4.0 metres tall (the average is still 1.75). We might feel a little cheated if one turned out to be a babe in arms and the remainder all approaching 2.00 metres, and foolish for not realising that the group might consist of five women and five men, with the group of women significantly shorter than the group of men.

The Sample

It is clear that the simple average is not sufficient to tell us all we need to know about the original set of numbers. Furthermore, the average of the set we have is not necessarily the average of all the possible numbers from which the set was taken. In the example of heights, we have deduced various "facts", probably erroneously, because the average is roughly what we had expected the average height of all people (past, present and future), to be. If the average height of the people outside the room had been say 1.25 metres or 2.25 metres, we would have been far less surprised to have seen a group of unusual heights enter.

Any set of numbers, be they heights or otherwise, are representatives of a much larger set of numbers that the mathematician assumes to be infinite but which are clearly not. There has not been, and will not be, an infinite number of people born, but in a practical sense the number is large enough for us to consider it as infinite. To illustrate the concept of infinity further, imagine that you were to count all the grains of sand on a beach, then on every beach in the British Isles, then Europe, then the World. When you had finished (assuming you were to live that long!) you would know precisely how many grains of sand there were in the world and it would be a finite number.

One reason why the mathematician assumes the full set of numbers (the population as it is called) to be infinite is so that he can say that there exists just one number which is *the* average of the population. Whenever a sample is taken from the population, just as we took the ten people who stood outside the door, the average of that sample is an estimate of what the true average of the whole population really is. It is a sampling of the average taken from the sample of the population. The greater the number of items, or observations, in the sample, the closer we would expect to be to the real average of the population, but we cannot rely upon it. We may have been unlucky enough to pick for our large sample all the big ones or all the small ones, thus giving a distorted picture.

How are we to tell how close the average we have calculated is to the true average? All through we have used words such as "most likely", "expected", "estimate" and "perhaps". These words suggest a level of confidence (or even lack of it) in how far we believe the average of the sample to be representative of the whole. It is necessary to quantify that level of confidence and to apply a percentage confidence, obviously less than one hundred, but greater than zero.

So far we have calculated an average of a sample and found that it has given us information, albeit limited information, about that sample, and even more limited information about the population as a whole. We might therefore ask whether taking an average is the most sensible action to take, since what we would truly like to do is to represent the whole by just one number, if we posssibly could. There is nothing particulary sacred about an average: in fact various kinds of average have been invented, e.g. harmonic, geometric and the one we have been using, the arithmetic. There are also the median, the mode, the quartiles and other such measures, but none are as convenient to use mathematically as the arithmetic mean (we called it average), we have so far described. Perhaps there is still scope for further invention!

Variation

Given the average value then, we have seen that the elements from which that average is made up may be close to the average, may be equally balanced on either side but at the extremes, and may be distributed anywhere in between. It would be helpful therefore if we could devise some means by which the dispersion could be measured. Fortunately such a measure does exist.

Each element, or observation, deviates from the average either positively or negatively (there may be observations which are the same as the average and therefore deviate by zero, but we shall assume these to be positive). Since we should like to record the extent of the deviations, we might consider summing all the deviations, positive and negative, and let this represent the deviation about the average of the observations in the sample. A simple check will illustrate that if this were done, the result would always be zero, whatever the dispersion within the sample about the average. However, if the deviations were firstly squared, thus producing all positive numbers since the square of a negative number is always postive, and then summed, the resulting number would be small if the observations were all close to the average and large if widely dispersed. As a refinement, we might divide by the number of observations in the sample, and then take the square root of the result.

By adopting this process we can calculate what is known as the standard deviation.

In more mathematical form we can say that if x_1, x_2, x_3 ... x_{n-1}, x_n are numerical observations, then the mean of these numbers is:

$$\bar{x} = \frac{1}{n} \sum_{i=1}^{n} x_i$$

The variance is the sum of the squares of each observation subtracted from the mean, divided by n. Its formula is:

$$\sigma^2 = \frac{1}{n} \sum_{i=1}^{n} (\bar{x} - x_i)^2$$

The standard deviation is the square root of the variance:

$$\sigma = \sqrt{\left[\frac{\sum_{i=1}^{n} (\bar{x} - x_i)^2}{n} \right]}$$

The average and the standard deviation shown in mathematical form above are just two numbers which have been so calculated to provide considerable insight into all the observations in a sample without actually listing them all. If we return for a moment to our ten people outside the door and we now learn that their average height is still 1.75 metres and they also have a standard deviation of 0.01 metres, we can be confident enough that they are all roughly the same height.   Note however that really we have been told three items of information about the people outside: we also know how many of them there are. If there had been one hundred people outside with a standard deviation of 0.01, we should expect perhaps that although most of the heights would be near the average, one or two could be further afield, the effect of the deviation diminished by the large number of observations (i.e. divided by 100). The number of observations which lie within any given range about the average may be stated with a degree of confidence dependent upon the size of the range. This will become clearer later as we explain why it is necessary to look upon the standard deviation we have calculated as merely an estimate of the standard deviation of the whole population.

Normal Distribution

In 1773 Abraham De Moivre completed the development of the normal distribution curve, long before the study of statistics as we know it today had really begun. Yet the normal distribution function is one of the most important equations in statistics; it allows us to draw all kinds of sensible and rational conclusions from raw data, average and standard deviation, provided we do not abuse it.   The normal distribution is frequently known as the Gaussian distribution, named after the German mathematician Gauss.   In fact, Gauss was born some thirty years after De Moivre's death and later took the credit for rediscovering and applying it.

The shape of the normal distribution curve, "bell" shaped, is shown in Fig. 2. There is an equation which describes the curve in mathematical terms, which at first glance appears complicated. It is:

$$y = \frac{1}{\sqrt{(2\pi b)}} \ \exp\left[-\frac{1}{2}\left(\frac{x-a}{b}\right)^2\right]$$

The a and b are numbers fixed for any given curve, so that on the graphical representation we have in Fig. 2, the line of the "bell" shows how y is related to x for specific values of a and b, in fact 0 and 1 respectively.

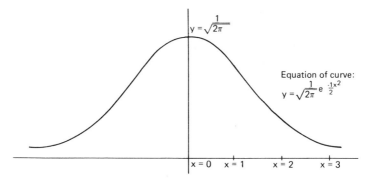

Fig. 2. Normal distribution curve, mean = 0, standard deviation = 1

Let us suppose that we have an infinite number of observations, x. Let us also suppose that different observations can have the same value, and that we know in advance how many x's there are of each different value, i.e. the frequency of occurrence of each possible value of x. Furthermore, x can lie anywhere between minus infinity and plus infinity; all values of x are possible, not just whole numbers, not just discrete fractions, but all values.

Let us now assume that one value of x, we shall call it x^1, occurs more frequently than any other: that values of x smaller than this number occur progressively less frequently. In fact, values of x equi-distant and on either side of x^1 have the same frequency of occurrence. If we now translate these suppositions into diagrammatic form, we produce a picture which is similar in nature to the normal distribution curve, where x is the value of the observation, and y is the frequency of its occurrence.

It follows that the observation with the greatest frequency of occurrence, i.e. the one in the middle, is the average of all observations. In Fig. 2, the value of x at this point is 0. If we were to slide the "bell" along to the right as shown in Fig. 3, that value of x would increase, in fact to 3. The actual equations of the curves are shown on each respective figure. Note that in the first, the a of the general formula above is equal to zero and that in the second it is equal to 3. These, of course, are the average values of the x's in each respective case. We may conclude therefore that, in the general formula, the value of a is always the average of all the observations, or x's, which that formula represents.

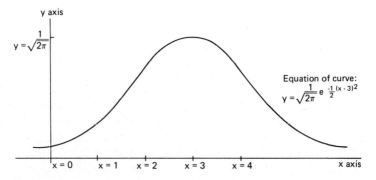

Fig. 3.   Normal distribution curve, mean = 3, standard deviation = 1

Area under the Curve. It happens to be a fact that, for the general normal distribution curve, if we take a slice of area under the curve from $x = a$ to $x = a+b$, 34.1% of the total area under the curve is contained (rounded to the nearest tenth). Figure 4 illustrates this point. From $x = a+b$ to $x = a+2b$ the area is 13.6%. Because the curve is symmetrical, the equivalent percentage areas are also contained on the other side of the $x = a$ line, as Fig. 4 shows. Note that this is an absolutely general statement: whatever the values of a and b, it is true. It is true in Figs. 2 and 3, as well as in Fig. 4.

There are many such relationships in mathematics, most of which are merely of academic interest. Not so this one.

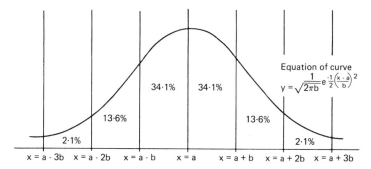

Fig. 4. Normal distribution, area under the curve

The *b* of the equation turns out to have a significance of major importance. If it were possible to carry out the standard deviation calculations described previously on all the observations, or *x*'s (remember there are an infinity of them!), about the average *a*, *b* would be the result. *b* is the standard deviation of the observations represented by the normal distribution curve.

What in reality does this mean? It means that, given a normal distribution, 34.1% of all the observations lie between their average and their average plus standard deviation, and so on. Put another way, if we know the average and the standard deviation of a normal distribution, we can be 68.2% sure that the next observation we encounter at random lies within one standard deviation of the average (34.1% either side).

Identifying the Source. Let us now turn the facts around and use them in a different way. Suppose we know the average and the standard deviation, and we have one observation to consider. We wish to know whether that observation has come from the distribution whose average and standard deviation we know. Clearly, any possible value of *x* could have come from the distribution, but some more likely than others. By using the relationships between average, standard deviation and area that we have discovered, we can identify the percentage probability that the observations comes from the distribution in question.

In the last paragraph we have dropped the use of the word "normal" in describing the distribution. This is a lapse, but common. In practice, we do not have truly normal distributions to consider, but they are approximately normal, and we assume them to be so. For example, we earlier discussed the heights of people. It is just within the bounds of the imagination that people, at birth, could be close to zero in height, but certainly not negative. Equally, twenty-feet tall would be out of the question. Yet we use the principles of the normal distribution to draw conclusions.

We are also unaware of the true average and standard deviation of all people. Nevertheless, we can make estimates, a most reasonable one being the average of the sample and the standard deviation. To be strictly accurate, to find the estimate of the standard deviation of the population we should divide by one less than the number of observations in the sample, not by the actual number in the sample, because the "one less" answer gives a better estimate of the true standard deviation of the normal distribution from which the sample is assumed to have come. The proof is beyond the scope of this book.

STATISTICS USED PROPERLY

So far we have merely scratched the surface of the methodology of statistics. There are many formulae and tests which have been devised to improve and measure various estimates derived from data. The objective is always to compress the data into few, manageable numbers which themselves are assumed to represent a particular curve form, or distribution. Once this is achieved, within probability confidence limits, further deductions may be made about the data without actual reference to it.

Statistics is relevant to Operational Research and an integral part of it because the collection of numerical data and subsequent analysis is essential. For the right conclusions to be drawn the O.R. worker must fully understand the methodology, implications and limitations of statistical analysis. It has been said that there are "lies, damn lies and statistics", but not in the hands of the conscientious and skilled analyst who measures and declares at all times the confidence he places on the results of his findings.

DISCUSSION QUESTIONS

1. What is the difference between descriptive statistics and the statistics used by the Operational Research practitioner?

2. Given the temperatures on a particular day in June for the past fifty years, how many numbers, or statistics, would reasonably represent that data and what would those numbers be called? How should the data be interpreted?

3. Write down a set of twenty numbers. Calculate the arithmetic mean, the variance and the standard deviation. Investigate how changes in the data affect these three values.

4. Consider the general formula for the normal distribution curve. How does the shape of the curve change if b, the standard deviation, is increased? What happens if b decreases? Interpret these results using real data.

5. Given a normal distribution with mean 3 and standard deviation 2, write down its formula. What percentage of all the observations will lie between one and five?

6. How should statistical data be treated? In what way may conclusions be drawn?

CHAPTER IV

Statistics - the Practice

A DISTRIBUTION PROBLEM

We have discussed the basic concepts of statistics in Chapter III. To illustrate how they might be used, let us consider a food distributor who is becoming increasingly anxious about the time his vehicles spend in long delivery delays at certain stores. Perhaps because of special stock-checking procedures, insufficient space or simply slow workers, the goods are not being taken off the vehicles fast enough, queues form and vehicles wait. This affects the whole day's delivery schedule and other customers suffer. The distributor may take a number of courses of action to correct the situation. They range from discontinuing supply to the offending customers (difficult to do if they account for a large part of the company's business), calling at times when it is known the queues are shortest, to making special appointments with the customers to ensure that the goods are taken at specified times.

Each of these proposals has its difficulties as well as its advantages. An alternative solution is to accept the situation as it is and build in to the total journey time of the delivery vehicle a contingency factor for queueing. In other words, when planning the delivery route and deciding on how many customers each individual vehicle should call, additional time should be included for delay. But how much?

Collecting and Analysing the Data

The first step is to ask each delivery man to record how long he spent at each customer waiting for his turn to unload. For simplicity we shall assume that the data so obtained is of sufficient accuracy, but in practice careful checks would need to be made to ensure that it gave a true picture of what was actually happening at the customer delivery points. After several observations have been recorded we can analyse the data in a formal way and calculate the mean of the delay times at all the customers. We could decide that this value, multiplied by the number of calls made on each journey, is the contingency factor for delay which should be included in the total journey time for each vehicle; but there are two main difficulties. The first is that the mean of delay time over all customers may not give a representative picture for each individual customer; this may be overcome by forming the mean of delay time for each customer and using these figures in our calculations instead of the one. The second difficulty is of more significance in that we can with considerable confidence say that on very few occasions will the mean delay time actually occur; at most times the total journey time will still be different from that which it was planned to be.

To illustrate the point further, there are two possible extreme cases. The delivery man finds at one customer that there are always at least three vehicles waiting when he arrives, but seldom more than five. At another customer it is just as likely that there will be no delay at all as there will be eight vehicles already waiting their turn to unload. Both customers have the same average delay time, but each have different characteristics. It would probably be wrong to serve one's most important customer after the second of the two examples above because it would not be possible to state with reasonable certainty at what time of the day that delivery would occur: only the variation in waiting time in the first of the two examples could be tolerated. We must therefore consider the variation in the data as well as the mean.

Degrees of Confidence

As we have seen in Chaper III, we can calculate a statistical measure known as variance, from which we can determine the standard deviation. Knowledge of the standard deviation tells us what degree of confidence we can have in the delay time we have so far determined by taking a simple mean. By assuming that expected delay time is equal to the mean, some delay times will be more reliably represented in practice than others; the larger the variance, the greater the variation in delay time. It is therefore useful to know how much confidence we can place in a delay time and how much safety margin we should employ to ensure that for a pre-arranged percentage of occasions the vehicle is able to move on to its next customer within a given time.

By using mathematical formulae derived from the equations of the normal distribution we can state precisely the probability that the delay time at a particular customer will not exceed a given amount. This means that management can decide in advance that it is willing to overrun scheduled journey times for say up to five per cent of all vehicles each day; the five per cent indicates that the delay time that is to be set for each customer must be such that the probability of achieving it is ninety-five per cent.

It would be wise to monitor the actual journey times to see that only five per cent of them do exceed plan. If more than five per cent consistently do so, it is likely that the customers are taking their deliveries in a significantly different way from that on which the original calculations were based. One might draw the same conclusion if a performance better than five per cent were achieved, even though the delivery men were receiving justifiable congratulations. If it is management policy to tolerate a five per cent overrun then it could be just as wrong to do better as it is to do worse.

Consideration of Other Factors

The total time spent with a customer is due to a number of factors such as waiting time, unloading, whether it is morning or afternoon, and so on. Unloading time will depend upon the type and quantity of goods being delivered. In some cases it is therefore appropriate to consider all of these factors instead of their total as discussed above. This can be achieved with the aid of linear regression which is a statistical technique for determining the effect of many factors on final outcome and is described more fully under forecasting in the next chapter. If we were able to collect the data categorised in this way, if it were accurate and if we were confident that the final result we achieved would be better than simply considering total time – and it is reasonable to express doubts on each of these counts – we could calculate the journey time of each vehicle as a function of its load, the characteristics of its customers and perhaps even of its driver. We shall not pursue this line any further here, but we should bear in mind that this kind of data and the statistical techniques we have discussed are of considerable importance in conducting simulation studies, which is the subject of Chapter VII.

DISCUSSION QUESTIONS

1. What are the difficulties involved in obtaining accurate and relevant data?

2. What is the practical value of the standard deviation?

3. How would we make use of the attributes of the normal distribution equation?

4. Is it reasonable and appropriate to identify one part of an overall problem and consider that part in isolation from the rest?

CHAPTER V

Forecasting and the Control of Stock

FORECASTING, PREDICTION AND TARGETS

Every company, even the most stable and the most confident of its market, must at least at one time in the year wish to make forecasts, be they forecasts of sales, raw materials usage, labour requirements or profit projections. From the marketing department's estimate of sales for the year, it is possible to calculate production schedules and distribution needs and from these to determine likely profits. At this stage, the forecasts which were originally made by the marketing department become objectives or targets and although the more recent the data the more accurate a forecast based on that data is likely to be, targets set some months in advance may not be changed except under extreme conditions and so marketing action, perhaps special advertising or promotions, must be taken to influence sales and keep them on target. Industrial companies, as opposed to those which are consumer goods orientated, are less likely to be able to change the course of sales at short notice in this way; any discrepancy in forecasts therefore means a corresponding discrepancy in profits.

A forecast is based on calculations performed on past data. Confusion sometimes exists when, on the record of sales performance, it is evident that targets cannot be met, yet the target is still looked upon as the forecast. If special attention is taken to change the natural course of sales, by which is meant the extrapolation of past data into the future, then the forecast must be overruled by means of a prediction. In the case of sales, this is normally provided by marketing. A prediction takes account of factors which are known only to those who are applying them. It must be treated with some trepidation since it is a human failing to show excesses of optimism if the prediction is for some long time in the future, and to become increasingly pessimistic as the time draws near.

Seasonality and Sales Cycles

It is possible in most companies to obtain data on past sales for periods of say one week over the previous two or three years. Such data is useful in helping to identify whether there are any seasonal influences on sales which can then be taken into account when making forecasts. There may be some evidence of sales cycles which are not in phase with the seasons and it may be possible to identify sales trends, either up or down. What will be clear is that sales will not conform to a smooth pattern — there will be fluctuations from week to week which cannot be explained by seasonality, cycles or trends and which can only be described as noise or random effect. It may not be totally random and doubtless if sufficient research were done reasons could be found, such as competitive activity or perhaps an absorbing television programme which stopped most people shopping at a particular time, but for all practical purposes, effects such as these may be considered to be random.

A further factor which must be borne in mind is that sales data is not necessarily demand since an out-of-stock situation will mean that demand cannot be satisfied. Customers may be willing to wait until stocks are replenished, but usually if demand cannot be satisfied immediately, it may be assumed to be lost.

Averages

A simple method of forecasting is to take an average of past data and to use this as the forecast of sales. It may be improved by taking a fixed number of weeks' past sales and as each new week passes to include that week in the average, and to drop the one which is the furthest back. This is known as a moving average. If it is thought that the most recent week is of more importance than the week earlier and that week more important than the week before and so on back to the earliest week included in the average, and if the weeks' sales are multiplied in that order by decreasing factors, the forecast so obtained is said to be a weighted moving average. The forecasts obtained by using the three kinds of average, described by arithmetical example in Table I, may be improved further by taking account of seasonality, trends and cycles, if they have been identified.

TABLE I: SIMPLE FORECASTING METHODS

Week no.	1	2	3	4	5	6	7	8	9	10 (now)	Next week
Sales data											
Sales	204	182	196	210	171	179	220	218	241	217	?

Simple average	*Moving average*	*Weighted moving average*
Total sales over all available weeks	Three-week moving average for week 4	Factors applied to
2,038	$\dfrac{204 + 182 + 196}{3} = 194$	this week: 3
Average sales 203.8	for week 5	last week: 2
Forecast sales	$\dfrac{182 + 196 + 210}{3} = 196$	week before: 1
for next week 204		
		Three-week weighted moving average
	for week 9	for week 9
	$\dfrac{179 + 220 + 218}{3}$	$\dfrac{179 \times 1 + 220 \times 2 + 218 \times 3}{6}$
	$= 205 \tfrac{2}{3}$	$= 212 \tfrac{1}{6}$
	for week 10	for week 10
	$\dfrac{220 + 218 + 241}{3}$	$\dfrac{220 \times 1 + 218 \times 2 + 241 \times 3}{6}$
	$= 226 \tfrac{1}{3}$	$= 229 \tfrac{5}{6}$
	for next week	for next week
	$\dfrac{218 + 241 + 217}{3}$	$\dfrac{218 \times 1 + 241 \times 2 + 217 \times 3}{6}$
	$= 225 \tfrac{1}{3}$	$= 226 \tfrac{1}{6}$
	Forecast sales for next week 226	Forecast sales for next week 227

Exponential Smoothing

A most common method of forecasting is known as exponential smoothing. In its simplest form it consists of taking the forecast made for the week just ended and adding to that forecast a proportion, usually one-tenth, of the difference between what actually happened and that week's forecast. In mathematical form:

$$NWF = TWF + 0.1\ (AS - TWF)$$

where NWF is next week's forecast, TWF is the forecast for the week just ended and AS is actual sales. This week's forecast (TWF) will have been derived in a similar way from the forecast for the previous week and the sales in that previous week, as will have been forecasts in all weeks prior to that. This means that exponential smoothing takes account of sales data in earlier weeks and is in effect a form of the weighted moving average with the major advantage that only the last week's forecast need be remembered. Tables II and III illustrate the methodology of exponential smoothing, using the data of Table I.

TABLE II: SALES DATA

	Week no.	1	2	3	4	5	6	7	8	9	10 (now)	Next week
Sales data	Sales	204	182	196	210	171	179	220	218	241	217	?

Exponential smoothing formula:
    next week's forecast = this week's forecast + 0.1 x (actual sales − this week's forecast)
Assume that the sales estimate for week 1 (before week 1 sales are known) = 200
Then forecast for week 2 = 200 + 0.1 x (204 − 200) = 200.4 (applying the exponential smoothing formula)

Linear Regression

Another method of forecasting is by linear regression. This means identifying the straight line which passes through a set of points on a graph so that it is the best fit,

TABLE III: EXPONENTIAL SMOOTHING

Week no.	This week's forecast	Actual sales minus this week's forecast	Next week's forecast
2	201	$182 - 201 = -19$	199.1
3	200	$196 - 200 = -4$	199.6
4	200	$210 - 200 = -10$	201.0
5	201	$171 - 201 = -30$	198.0
6	198	$179 - 198 = -19$	196.1
7	197	$220 - 197 = -23$	199.3
8	200	$218 - 200 = -18$	201.8
9	202	$241 - 202 = 39$	205.9
10	206	$217 - 206 = 11$	207.1
Next week	208		

Note. To simplify the arithmetic, this week's forecast is increased to the next highest whole number.

as illustrated in Fig. 5. In that example, "best fit" means the line which passes at each point in time through the sales quantities, which, when measured from actual sales at those times, provides differences, the sum of squares of which is a minimum.

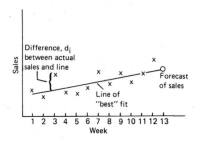

Fig. 5. Linear regression

In more mathematical form, d_i as shown in Fig. 5 is defined as the difference in week i between actual sales in week i and the sales which would have occurred in week i if sales had been on the line of best fit. The line of best fit takes the form

$$sales = a . \ time + b$$

where a and b are constants which determine where the line is placed in relation to the sales in each week. The line satisfies the condition that the sum of the d_is squared is a minimum, i.e. Σd_i^2 is minimum.

The values of a and b can be found from:

$$a = \frac{\Sigma t_i s_i - w\bar{t}.\bar{s}}{\Sigma t_i^2 - w\bar{t}^2}$$

and

$$b = \bar{s} - a\bar{t}$$

where $\bar{t}$ and $\bar{s}$ are the averages of time and sales respectively, w is the number of weeks, t_i and s_i are week number and sales in week i respectively and Σ means form the sum of the terms immediately following for all weeks.

Once the line has been determined, using the formulae above for a and b, the forecast is said to be the sales quantity on the line for the next time period ahead. But linear regression need not only be restricted to measuring variation against time, as Table IV illustrates. Instead of t representing time, it could be, for example, the amount of money in thousands of pounds spent on advertising in previous years.

TABLE IV: EXAMPLE OF REGRESSION ANALYSIS

Advertising expenditure (t)	Sales (s)	$t_i s_i$	t_1^2	
2	60	120	4	Show $a = 8$
3	80	240	9	
4	70	280	16	and $b = 48$
5	100	500	25	
6	90	540	36	

STOCK CONTROL

Economic Order Quantity

If all forecasts were accurate (and we can be sure that they rarely are) stock control would be a simple matter of maintaining levels of stock determined by an exact knowledge of future demand. A balance would be needed between keeping *(a)* too much stock, which is costly in space, tied capital, insurance and other elements, and *(b)* too little, with consequent frequent ordering and handling of goods, which can be expensive. A formula which goes some way to achieving the balance is known as the economic order quantity or E.O.Q. and is expressed:

$$\text{E.O.Q.} = \sqrt{\frac{2AS}{R}}$$

where A is the annual sales, S is the cost of ordering and R is the cost of holding an item in stock for one year. It is derived by equating the cost of ordering a regular quantity X to the cost of holding in stock that same quantity X, where the costs of ordering and holding are expressed on the left-hand and the right-hand sides of the equation respectively:

$$\frac{A}{X} \cdot S = \tfrac{1}{2}XR$$

A/X represents the number of times in one year that an order is placed and the $\tfrac{1}{2}X$ on the right-hand side is the average quantity in stock during the year.

It is assumed that sales demand is steady and known precisely, which means that orders of the same quantity can be placed at regular intervals. It applies only to stock in discrete lots, either raw materials or finished goods, and has no relevance to work in progress. A formula such as this is useful only where the stockholder has no interest whatsoever in the costs incurred by the supplier. It is therefore appropriate for a wholesaling operation. If however it is necessary to consider the costs of manufacture, or include the costs of holding the goods in a central location before they are supplied to a local depot, the problem becomes more involved. In the case of the manufacturer, he is concerned to make full and economic use of his plant and machinery and therefore wishes to produce batch quantities which minimise unit costs. These economic manufacturing quantities, E.M.Q.s, are not necessarily compatible with the E.O.Q.s, but may be made to be so.

Safety Stock

Sales demand is never as steady as one would like and accordingly it is worthwhile to record by how much actual sales differ from forecast. If sufficient data is collected, it is possible to say how frequently in the past sales and forecasts have differed by given amounts; from these figures, probabilities of the difference exceeding certain amounts in the future can be expressed. It can be seen that this approach is similar to that adopted when taking the average of a set of observations and then calculating their standard deviations as discussed in Chapter III. If now it is agreed by management that say ninety five per cent of the time there should be stock available to satisfy demand (stock to satisfy one hundred per cent of demand would mean infinite quantities) it is a relatively simple matter to hold additional stock over and above forecast such that the probability of sales exceeding forecast plus that additional stock is just five per cent. The additional stock is known as safety or buffer stock and the management decision on frequency of stockouts is their choice of service level to their customers.

DISCUSSION QUESTIONS

1. Why should a company make forecasts?

2. What is the difference between a forecast and a target?

3. What are the factors which contribute towards a forecast?

4. Why is exponential smoothing a popular method of forecasting?

5. What are the shortcomings of linear regression as a means of forecasting?

6. How are inaccuracies in forecasting countered when applied to the control of stock?

CHAPTER VI

The Theory of Queues

THE OCCURRENCE OF QUEUES

Queues are a common occurrence in everyday life. Perhaps the first queue situation which springs to mind is that which takes place at the check-out desk of a super-market. One of the main reasons for the growth in popu-larity of the supermarket and decline of the so-called corner-shop store has been an awareness on the part of the shopper that considerable savings in time can be made if one's shopping may be gathered personally from the super-market shelves instead of asking the shop assistant for every single item — assuming of course that the goods one wants can readily be found on the shelves. Because of this emphasis on time saving, when the shopper arrives at the check-out desk he or she is much more aware of the time it takes to stand in line waiting for the goods to be checked so that the money may be paid and the goods purchased. The supermarket manager is anxious therefore to provide a quick check-out service, but is equally concerned that the cost of doing so should not be exorbi-tant.

Ships waiting to enter a harbour are not unlike shoppers waiting in a queue to pay their bills before leaving the supermarket with their purchases. Ships suffer the same kinds of problems because they arrive at the port in an irregular fashion, i.e. not according to a rigid predeter-mined schedule. The requirement of the ship is to be unloaded and/or loaded as quickly as possible so that the ship owners may get the greatest return from their investment in the ship itself and from the crew they employ. It is important therefore that the dockers at the berths should carry out their tasks quickly and efficiently. A ship idling outside a port and waiting for entry can be very costly and this must be balanced against the cost of providing better facilities in the form of a larger number of, and more efficient, berths.

It is frustrating when using the telephone to find that the person whom one is trying to call is continuously engaged. If the person one wishes to contact is already speaking on his own line there is little that can be done other than wait until the line clears. Sometimes, however, the reason for the engaged tone is that the telephone switching equipment in the telephone exchange is busy, not the subscriber himself whom one is calling. When a number is dialled on the telephone, a great deal of activity takes place in the telephone exchanges. Every subscriber does not have his own personal line to every other subscriber, and so facilities have to be shared. This being so, a particular piece of equipment may already be servicing an existing conversation, so that when one's dialling activity reaches that stage of the connection the line is found to be busy and the call cannot be made. For obvious reasons of cost, the Post Office does not allow calls which have reached the busy stage to queue although technically it is possible for them to do so. The subscriber must wait a while and attempt to make the call again later. This situation is of interest to us, however, because again we have identified a facility which is required to service a customer. To run an efficient organisation, the Post Office must decide just how many of each facility it will provide to ensure an appropriate level of customer satisfaction.

Queue Characteristics

We have given three examples above of how queues might form. We might cite many more examples, but we will most probably find that they will not be much different in character from the examples we have already given. The queue that forms at the factory store is not dissimilar to that which occurs at the supermarket check-out desk. Neither is the body of cars waiting to take up the next available car park space much different from the ships waiting to enter harbour. From the Operational Research standpoint all these problems are the same.

The object of the exercise is to provide a service always at an acceptable cost; to satisfy the needs of the members of the queue without spending too much on the facilities which serve them. In the case of the supermarket, the more check-out points there are the more it costs in manning, provision of tills, and utilisation of space which might otherwise be used to display more goods; yet with too few check-out points customers might well decide to buy their goods elsewhere.

In attempting to reconcile these opposing constraints, we must first collect data that represents the queueing situation we are about to analyse. There are two principal items of information that we must have, the first is the manner in which people (in the case of ports it would of course be ships) join the queue, and the second is the way in which the customers are processed through the check-out desk (again, in the case of ships it would be loaded/unloaded at the berths). By "manner" and "way" we mean information such as average arrival rate and arrival of newcomers to the queue and the expected duration at any time before the customer currently being served is finally dealt with. We should also need to know whether the length of the queue has any influence upon customer willingness to join it, whether one particular check-out point has a greater customer attraction than any other, or whether there is an upper limit, i.e. cut-off point, on queue length. It will be seen that, in these mathematical terms, the only differences between supermarket, port and tele-phone exchange are the numerical values of the parameters which define them. The basic characteristics of them all are the same.

Queue Control

If we are able to take queue characteristics and treat them in a mathematical fashion, we need to know first on what criteria a solution to the queueing problem will be judged: indeed, we must know more clearly what it is that the person in control of the queue is really trying to achieve. No matter how many check-out points are installed, there will always remain the possibility that so many customers will arrive at a given time that the supermarket will be swamped and hence keep customers waiting to pay their bills for longer than might be thought desirable. We must therefore look for a solution to the problem which provides for customers waiting on average for no longer than a given time, and for a queue to be of a given average length. Additionally, we must bear in mind that the behaviour of a queue is very much dependent, at least in the early stages, upon its starting conditions. If, for example, many people have already formed a queue before the check-out desk comes into operation, the check-out girl will be hard pressed to reduce the length of that queue. Nevertheless, she will succeed eventually in doing so and therefore, no matter what the starting conditions might be, the length of the queue and the waiting time that an individual will expect to remain in it, will settle down to particular values.

MATHEMATICAL ANALYSIS

The mathematics of the theory of queues is somewhat complex, yet it is recognised that the mathematical equations which are developed rarely represent a real-life queueing situation. The reason for this is the necessity to make stringent assumptions about the behaviour of queues under study so that the mathematical techniques which we are able to apply can actually be used. This may sound a defeatist statement, but a great deal can be learnt about the behaviour of queues from mathematical analysis, even though the results of such a study may not always be directly applicable. The Operational Research scientist does not of course allow the matter to rest there; to solve a queueing problem truly, he adopts the process of solution known as simulation, about which we shall say more in the next chapter.

The mathematical analysis begins by assuming that, over a very small interval of time, the probability that no one will join the queue is very high, the probability that one person will join the queue is small, and that the probability that more than one person will join the queue is negligible. Those readers who have an understanding of statistics will realise that the assumptions we have made are precisely those which generate a Poisson distribution. Although such an awareness is useful in further analysis, it is not important to our basic understanding of the problem.

The next assumption we make is that, whenever a customer is being served, the probability that the service will not be completed over a very short time interval is high, and that the probability of completion of service in the same small interval of time is very small. Given these assumptions, it is now possible to write down the relationships between them.

Before we do so, however, we must firstly decide what values to give to the "high probability" of no one joining the queue and the "high probability" of the service not being completed. These values are taken to be the average arrival rate and the reciprocal of the time it takes to serve a customer, respectively.

We now determine a number of equations which relate the current queue length to its previous states. Taking the state of the queue in a most general form, we consider the probability that there are n customers in the queue. This situation could have arisen as follows:

1. $n - 1$ people in the queue and 1 arrival;
2. $n + 1$ people in the queue and 1 service completed;
3. n people in the queue, 1 arrival and 1 service completed;

4. $n - 2$ people in the queue and 2 arrivals;
and so on.

It will be seen that all we are doing is writing down all possible ways in which a queue of n people could be formed from all possible previous states. Fortunately, most previous states need not be considered because we have initially made the assumption that the probability of two or more people joining the queue within a small time interval or two or more people completing service within the same small time interval is negligible. We can therefore exclude from consideration all previous states which have queue lengths other than $n - 1$, n or $n + 1$. We are then in a position to write the probability equation as follows: the probability that there will be n people in the queue at a given point in time is related to (a) the probability that there will be $n - 1$ people in the queue in the previous time interval, (b) the probability that there will be n people in the queue in the previous time interval, and (c) the probability that there will likewise have been $n + 1$ people.

From such an equation can be developed a variety of facts about the behaviour of the queue. It is not the intention of this book to explore the mathematics in depth; we shall instead provide the derived formulae which describe the characteristics of the queue.

Some Queue Equations

The simplest queueing situation consists of one service channel, the units in the queue served strictly in the order of arrival, each unit treated in identical fashion and no limit to the queue length. The probability of the arrival of a unit to join the queue and the probability of the unit which is being served completing that service are each independent of time or the state of the system. In other words, it is just as likely that the next unit will arrive, whether the queue length be short or long and whatever the time of day. Similarly, a unit which has been undergoing service for some time has the same likelihood of completing that service within a given time as another unit which has only just started its service.

With these restrictions in mind, it is possible to derive mathematical formulae for the behaviour of queues. The constant probability of occurrence implies a Poisson distribution of the events and an exponential distribution of intervals between events. If the average rate of arrival of units is λ in unit time, and dt is taken to be a very small interval of time, then:

1. the probability of one arrival between times t and $t + dt$ is:

$$\lambda dt$$

2. the probability of n arrivals in time t is

$$\frac{1}{n!} (\lambda t)^n e^{-\lambda t}$$

3. the probability of an interval between t and $t + dt$, before the next arrival is:

$$\lambda e^{-\lambda t} dt$$

4. the probability of an interval greater than t is

$$e^{-bt}$$

5. the average interval between arrivals is

$$\frac{1}{\lambda}$$

If the average service time is $1/\mu$, 1. to 5. above apply to completion of service with μ substituted for λ. For example, in 3., the probability of an interval between t and $t + dt$ before service is completed is $\mu e^{-\mu t} dt$, provided the service channel is busy — otherwise it is zero.

The mathematical techniques to arrive at a solution use differential difference equations (other ways are possible). We exemplify the results by considering a supermarket operation with one cashier — we assume that the rate of customer arrival remains the same throughout the day although this is unlikely to be so in practice.

On average, nine customers arrive every five minutes

and the cashier can serve ten in five minutes. Then $\lambda = 1.8$, $\mu = 2.0$ and $\rho = 0.9$, where $\rho = \lambda/\mu$ is defined as the traffic intensity.

We now calculate that:

1. the average number of customers waiting for service is:

$$Q = \rho^2/(1 - \rho) = 0.81/0.1 = 8.1$$

2. the probability that the queue will be greater than ten people is:

$$P(>10) = \rho^{n+1} = (0.9)^{11} = 0.31$$

    i.e. 31% of the time the queue will be greater than ten.

3. the probability that a customer may have to wait longer than two minutes for service is:

$$w(>2) = \rho e^{-2(\mu-\lambda)} = 0.9e^{-2 \times 0.2} = 0.60$$

It may be possible to speed up service to twelve in five minutes by relocating the cashier in the store. In which case,

$$\lambda = 1.8, \mu = 2.4 \text{ and } \rho = 0.75$$

The effects on Q, P and w are:

1. $Q = 0.5625/0.25 = 2.25$
2. $P(>10) = (0.75)^{11} = 0.042$
3. $w(>2) = 0.75e^{-1.2} = 0.23$

which is a significant improvement in service to the customer.

DISCUSSION QUESTIONS

1. What are queues and when do they occur?
2. What are the principal characteristics of queues?
3. What are the objectives of queue control?
4. How useful in a practical sense is queueing theory?

CHAPTER VII

Simulation

MODELLING

People make models for a great variety of reasons. We usually think of models as small replicas of life-size objects, for example, the model car, the doll, or various kinds of ornaments. The majority of models tend to be made for decorative purposes, or as toys, or to provide us with a degree of pleasure and enjoyment. Nevertheless, there are other types of model which have functional purposes as well, and some which are built solely to investigate how a particular design or operation might work, without any regard to the general appearance of the model.

In the category of models, which are both functional and attractive, we might include stage "props". Another example might be the model of a complete town, or of a company's prestigious new office block. It is far easier to appreciate the advantages and shortcomings of a planned building if one is able to see a three-dimensional model of it before it is constructed. It might be argued that with sufficient imagination it would be possible to realise fully what the building will eventually look like from the basic architectural drawings and the plans. But the purpose of the model is to have a better understanding of the total view of the design, especially the relationships of one part of the building to another.

The construction company with a contract to build a new harbour would be foolish if it did not take into account tidal conditions, the importance of building harbour walls in the most effective places, and the purpose for which the harbour was to be built. Unfortunately however, until the harbour is finally constructed, it is not possible to know whether the harbour will perform as well as was intended. One way out of this dilemma is to build a much smaller version of the harbour, to create artificially the conditions under which the harbour will operate (for example, wave patterns, tidal conditions, arrival and departure of shipping) and to observe the effect of these external influences on the structure. In a similar vein, models are usually made of aircraft before the prototype is built, and the model is subjected to stringent tests. Severe operating conditions are imposed upon the model in wind tunnels and by wing and fuselage stress experiments. The object of these tests is to identify any inherent weaknesses in the model, and hence in design, so that they may be corrected before the actual project is built. Clearly, such weakness would eventually be discovered even if a model had not in the first place been built, and presumably modifications could have been incorporated; but if faults in design do exist, it is usually cheaper and often safer to iron them out in the model stage rather than when the final product is in service.

Mathematical Models

We tend to expect models to have an appearance similar to that which they are designed to represent. We expect to recognise the model as a smaller version of the end product. In fact, it is not necessary in some cases to build a physical model at all; we can learn a great deal about the performance of an aircraft from mathematical equations which describe the structure of the aircraft and its relationship to external conditions, such as air flow. These equations in themselves could be considered to be a model of the aircraft, and a great deal of time, effort and cost can be avoided by judicious use of mathematics. Nevertheless, in the case of aircraft design, it would be unusual to rely solely upon the mathematics, and at a particular stage of design a model will be built.

But there are other kinds of mathematical models. Let us assume that a very large factory acts as a central distribution point for several smaller satellite factories. Heavy vehicles continuously arrive with goods from the satellites and other vehicles leave to supply depots throughout the country. Congestion frequently occurs, resulting in delays in supplying goods to the depots and hence to customers. There are a number of possible ways in which the factory and distribution centre could be organised and management wishes to choose the one which allows the smoothest operation.

A way of tackling the problem is to observe how frequently the vehicles arrive and depart, build a scale model of each possible layout, and try to copy or simulate the movements in miniature. Although models of vehicles and factory premises are pleasing to see, it quickly becomes apparent that to describe them in too great a detail is time consuming and wasteful − as much can be learnt by manipulating matchboxes representing lorries around outline drawings of buildings as can be learnt by using exact models. Provided there is sufficient space, it is not the physical characteristics of the vehicles and of the buildings which matter, but the time it takes for each vehicle to carry out a series of well defined movements and procedures. We may focus our attention upon considerations of time, delays, waiting and congestion so that the model need no longer be a tangible three-dimensional one, but instead a listing of times that it takes for the vehicles to perform specific tasks, the frequency with which they arrive and depart, the variations in these times and the relationships between the tasks.

The factory distribution point has therefore been reduced to a set of mathematical relationships. We are concerned solely with the problems of congestion, not with the aesthetic beauty of the eventual factory layout that we shall choose. However, if we had built a conventional model of the system, it would be obvious how we might change the layout to reduce congestion and improve efficiency. We allow the mathematical model to change in a similar way, so that other layouts might be considered. For example, in one layout the vehicles may be routed in one direction and unloaded in the order in which they arrive, whilst in another they may be routed in an entirely different direction and unloaded in order of size of load.

Data Collection

The data we require to analyse the model, or perform the simulation as we might now call it, consists of information about how frequently service is required and how long that service takes when it is given. This is precisely the problem which was discussed in Chapter VI under queueing theory, but in that chapter we assumed that we knew the mathematical relationship between successive arrivals to join a queue, and the duration of service time. We also had a relatively simple queueing system, i.e. servers and queues requiring one particular function to be performed. We are now discussing a succession of queues, each of which does not necessarily behave according to the convenient mathematical way we assume in queueing theory. The methods of simulation are used in practice far more frequently than those of queueing theory.

To illustrate the kind of data collection that is required, we shall return again to the example of the factory with a central distribution point. We need to know facts such as the inter-arrival times of vehicles, and how long it takes to load and to unload them. If a distribution point were already in operation most of these facts might be culled from experience. Usually, however, the project under consideration is a new one and no actual running data is known. Even when there is some experience to fall back on, it must be remembered that, for example, the vehicle loading times might be related to the layout currently in operation.

Given a particular layout design, we decide in advance how frequently vehicles will arrive and how long it will take to service the requirements of the vehicles; we know load and unload times and how long it takes to manoeuvre vehicles into the correct position for loading/unloading. Rather than compile a list of such times it is often more convenient to assume that the duration between one activity and another can be sampled from a normal distribution. Computer programmes would be written to allow the whole analysis to take place, and sub-routines to provide sampling from the normal distribution are readily available.

Simulation Objectives

Several layouts of the distribution point can be tested, and eventually one chosen which is most appropriate to the needs of management. It is very important, therefore, for management to know what improvements in layout they are seeking and to have defined in advance which result from the simulation run is "best". As an example, it might be possible to reduce the average waiting time, i.e. the average time a vehicle spends waiting in the distribution centre, by rearranging the centre's facilities in some way. But this is of little value if, as a result, the departing vehicles do not have to wait at all and the arriving vehicles wait longer than before. The centre might soon run out of stock and, although there would be no delay for the vehicles feeding the depots, there might in time be no goods for them either.

We implied, when we first began to discuss the factory distribution point, that there was a problem of congestion. It is essential for us to define precisely what we mean by congestion, where it occurs, what is tolerable and what is not. For example, it might be acceptable for a given predetermined number of vehicles to queue to enter the factory, and we might wish them to experience no delay on departure. Yet it seems unlikely that we should be willing to tolerate queues entering the system unless they were contractors' vehicles for which we paid only for the distance travelled to deliver the goods. In this case, our concern would only be to ensure that the goods reached their destination at the earliest possible time, not necessarily to achieve maximum vehicle utilisation.

Just as with designing aircraft through the medium of a model, so we cannot be sure that the whole system will work before it is fully built and in operation. Nevertheless, we can learn a great deal about how the system will operate before we invest in costly buildings and procedures. We shall have been able to try out various possible schemes, and will have decided upon the one which is most appropriate to our needs.

AN EXAMPLE OF SIMULATION

We assume that vehicles laden with coal arrive at a china-clay works. They unload, the vehicles are washed and then loaded with clay for the return journey. Both on entry to and on exit from the yard, the vehicles and their contents are weighed. The average times taken at weighing, unloading, washing, loading and weighing again for departure are known, as well as the variation about that average. Only one vehicle at a time can be serviced by each facility and so queues form. The one weighbridge is shared by arriving and departing vehicles. Arriving vehicles are given priority if the unloading bay is vacant, otherwise the departing vehicle is weighed first. Times of arrival of vehicles have been noted and the time between successive arrivals are shown in Fig. 6.

The first vehicle arrives 10 minutes after the yard opens. It proceeds immediately to the weighbridge, thence to unload. Assuming average times spent at each facility, after 9 minutes of unloading, the second vehicle arrives. The weighbridge is free and after 5 minutes the first vehicle has moved on to be washed, allowing the second vehicle to move directly to unload. When the third vehicle arrives, the first has been in wash for 5 minutes and the second has been in unload for 3 minutes. When the fourth arrives, the weighbridge is free, but the third has

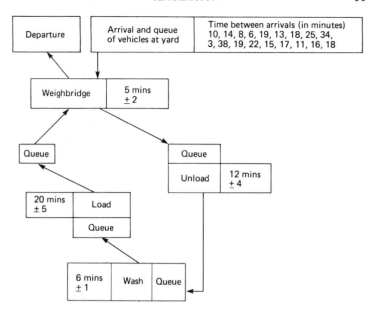

Fig. 6. An example of simulation

been queueing for one minute to unload, the second requires 3 minutes more to unload and the first has spent 5 minutes in loading. By the time the fifth vehicle arrives, the first vehicle has one more minute on the weighbridge before it departs and so the fifth must wait this time. In the meantime, the second is halfway through loading and the third has been in wash for 4 minutes. The fourth has been unloading also for 4 minutes, having waited 10 minutes for the third to move on to wash.

A log of times spent in queues may be kept, the maximum and average lengths of those queues, and the total times spent by the vehicles in the system. From this information it may be decided whether the facilities should be improved, for example whether two loading bays should be provided instead of one or two weighbridges. The effect on vehicle times in the system can be determined by running the same arrival data through the new system with the duplicate facilities. It may be made more realistic by varying the times taken in the facilities within the limits shown, and by imposing a travelling time between facilities of one minute or so.

DISCUSSION QUESTIONS

1. What is a model?

2. In what sense can mathematical equations be used to describe a model?

3. Why do we simulate?

4. What are the advantages of simulation compared with:
   (a) actually building the full-scale version of the model; and
   (b) adopting a more mathematically deterministic solution?

5. What are the disadvantages?

CHAPTER VIII

Linear Programming - the Concept

IDENTIFYING THE PROBLEM

The mechanics of solving a linear programming problem have been researched, tried and tested in great depth. However, before the mathematical analysis can be applied, the problem must first be identified as of a linear programming kind, and then be represented in mathematical form. A domestic example is discussed below to illustrate the principles.

Suppose that after a hard day at the office you decide to go home and relax in front of the TV set; the evening's programmes look good and you wish to enjoy the comforts of home. The TV set is on a bracket fixed to the wall and you intend to place your armchair in a suitable position in front of it. You suffer from eye strain if you sit too closely and, within the confines of the room, you would like to push your chair as far away as possible.

The central heating system in your house is particularly effective. So much so that to be too close to the radiator on the wall, which is opposite to the TV set, is positively uncomfortable. Unfortunately, there is a draught from the underneath of the door to the room which on many occasions you have decided to fix, but have not yet managed to do. You wish to keep far enough away from the radiator, out of the line of draught, and suitably placed to view the evening's entertainment.

To add to those hazards, a wall light hangs a little to one side of the TV set. The shade does not function as well as it should and there is a wedge of light which causes a glare, in front of which it is uncomfortable to sit. By suitably manoeuvring the armchair, you eventually find a place in the room to relax without suffering discomfort.

Let us now examine the various aspects of the situation in more detail and consider what was to have been achieved and what were the constraints imposed upon the solution. To assist in the analysis, we have a plan of the TV room in Fig. 7 which identifies the area of the room in

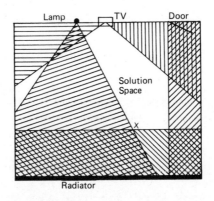

Fig. 7. TV watching — objectives and constraints

which the armchair might rest, and the position marked by a cross where the armchair finally is settled. The shaded parts show where there is too much warmth, a draught, a glare, or simply where the TV set cannot be seen. The only floor space on which the armchair may reside is that which is not shaded, and we call it the "solution space"

Objectives

Firstly we must decide what it is that we are trying to achieve, what is our objective, our objective function. In basic terms we might say that the objective is to watch television, but that might more readily have been achieved by calling in to the first public house on the way home from work. Clearly, if we had done that, other needs would not have been fulfilled, such as eating dinner at home before watching TV, or relaxing in one's own special armchair. When we express, therefore, a desire to watch TV, we take for granted that prior requirements should first be satisfied, without specifically saying so. In our own minds, "to watch TV" embraces all that we really mean, but to convey the idea to another, we have to be far more explicit.

But once we have reached home, dined, and about to settle down and relax, we encounter the additional problems, admittedly more localised, concerning the comfort rating of the various positions in which the armchair may be placed. It is clear that once we have reached the stage of entering the room, we are faced with a choice of *how* to watch TV, not just whether to do so or not. In which case, we must find some means of relating various factors so that the optimum siting for the armchair can be found. We want to be as far away as possible from the TV set, yet remain within the room and stay in line of vision. We wish to avoid glare, draught and excessive heat.

EXPRESSED MATHEMATICALLY

The objective function we are seeking may be expressed as "to be as far away from the TV set as possible". If we were to translate that objective function into mathematical terms, we would find it convenient to set the TV room as though one corner, the bottom left-hand corner, were at the origin of a graph with the bottom wall along the x axis and the left-hand wall along the y axis. Figure 8 illustrates this. Let us assume that the length of the room is 5 metres so that the top wall sits on the line $y=5$. The bottom wall is on $y=0$ and the left-hand wall on $x=0$.

"To be as far away from the TV set as possible" requires more explanation. Since the TV screen is parallel to the top wall ($y=5$), we shall assume that, given any particular line drawn within the room parallel to the top and bottom

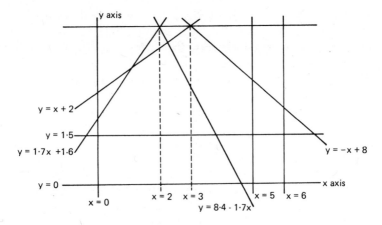

Fig. 8. TV watching — in graphical form

walls, any point on that line is equally desirable from which to watch the TV show. In reality that may not be so, and we shall return to discuss that matter later. Nevertheless, if we accept that any point on the line is equally desirable, we may say that our objective is to find the line, parallel to the top and bottom walls, which is the maximum distance from $y=5$. In other words, or in mathematical form, our solution is found when we have determined the line $y=Z$, such that Z is a minimum.

There are, however, other conditions or constraints to be taken into consideration. These are:

1. The possible lines from which the optimum solution may be found must all lie within the bounds of the room, i.e.:

$$y \leqslant 5, y \geqslant 0, x \leqslant 0, x \leqslant 6$$
(the room width is 6 metres)

2. The draught from the door runs at right angles to the closed door and follows the line $x = 5$. The viewer does not wish to sit in the draught and therefore is constrained to place his chair to the left of the line of draughts, i.e. in mathematical form:

$$x < 5$$

3. The radiator, which extends along the full length of the bottom wall, emits heat which is unbearable closer than 1.5 metres to it. This means keeping above the line $y = 1.5$, i.e.:

$$y \geqslant 1.5$$

4. The wall light is located on the top wall, 2 metres from the left-hand wall. Its glare covers a span of approximately 60 degrees. The lines which describe the extremities of the glare may be expressed as:

$$y = 1.7\,x + 1.6$$

and

$$y = 8.4 - 1.7x$$

So to avoid the glare we must site the armchair outside these two lines, i.e. either we choose:

$$y - 1.7x > 1.6$$
$$y + 1.7x > 8.4$$

5. The television set is placed right in the middle of the top wall. Its angle of vision is 90 degrees. The two equations of its extremities are therefore $y = x + 2$ and $y = -x + 8$. So to be in a position to watch TV, we need to be within these two lines, i.e.:

$$y - x \leqslant 2 \text{ and } y + x \leqslant 8$$

We might rewrite the problem purely in mathematical notation as follows:

Minimise the objective function $z\ (= y\ )$ subject to:

$$x \geqslant 0, x < 5, x \leqslant 6$$
$$y \geqslant 0, y \geqslant 1.5, y \leqslant 5$$
$$y\text{-}x \leqslant 2,$$
$$y+x \leqslant 8, y + 1.7x > 8.4$$

It will be seen that some constraints make others redundant, such as $x < 5$ predominating over $x \leqslant 6$. In addition, we have excluded the constraint $y - 1.7x > 1.6$ in order to be closer to the door (but still not in the draught).

Linearity

The equations used to describe the problem are all in linear form, that is neither x nor y are multiplied in any of the equations by anything other than a known arithmetic value: there are no xy's or x^2's. Further, when we described the problem diagrammatically, we found that every line we drew was straight. We have a problem which can be reduced to mathematical formulation in terms of linear inequalities with a linear objective function. It is this kind of problem that can be solved explicitly by means of the technique known as "linear programming". The process of solution is discussed in the next chapter, but before we proceed, there are still some useful observations we can draw from our TV-watching exercise.

Reality

Draught from a door does not necessarily flow in a straight line. Much more likely, the air currents will tend to curve, to push inwards into the main body of the room. It would not be difficult to write down a mathematical equation which would describe the extremities of such motion, but it would most certainly be non-linear. As we can see from Fig. 9, which illustrates such a hypothetical flow, the line is curved and therefore not linear.

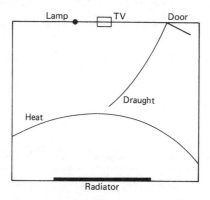

Fig. 9. TV watching — greater reality

In a similar fashion, the radiator will not cover the full extent of the bottom wall. It would be an unusual radiator if it did so. Much more likely it will cover a part of the wall and so emit heat which radiates as a curve from an elongated central point. Again Fig. 9 illustrates this.

The point of raising these issues is not to criticise the value of the method of solution we have adopted, but to be fully aware that we have made certain approximations. In reality, these approximations may not matter: the solution may turn out to be the same whether we make the equations linear or not. Unfortunately, as soon as we encounter non-linear equations, the solution becomes much more difficult to reach. There are suitable non-linear solution techniques for specific non-linear problems, but not a general method as there is for linear equations through the medium of linear programming..

The intensity of heat from the radiator diminishes the further we are away from it. It does not diminish in a linear way, but as we have described the problem, there is a threshold line on one side of which the heat is bearable, on the other side it is not. In this way we have legitimately created linearity out of non-linearity.

We might consider too the formulation of the objective function. As it stands, to position the armchair anywhere on the line $y = 1.5$, out of the glare and the draught, is a satisfactory answer. Yet it would not be unreasonable to assume that the best solution might be found closer to the glare than to the draught. The reason is so that the viewer can be more square to the TV set. We have not, however, taken the "squareness" into account, and if we did so it too would upset the linearity constraint. Nevertheless, it is possible to incorporate the "squareness" requirement by taking a common-sense view of how the problem might fall out when it is being formulatcd in the first place. The approach would be to define the objective function as the need to minimise $y + x$, instead of just y. The more mathematically inclined reader might like to determine the reason for himself.

Relaxing the Constraints

In attempting to site the armchair in the optimum place, we have tacitly accepted that all the constraints are fixed. Yet it would presumably have been possible to turn out the light, turn down the central heating system, move the television set or insulate the room more effectively. Each of these actions would have provided a means of solution to the problem which would have lessened the complexity of the linear programming formulation or would have avoided the necessity to use linear programming at all. These observations in this particular case appear trivial, yet when one considers other, real-life, applications of linear programming one may find that a closer look at the constraints will prove them to be less fixed than might at first be thought.

DISCUSSION QUESTIONS

1. What is an objective function and why is it needed?

2. Why is linear programming called "linear"? Illustrate mathematically and diagrammatically.

3. To what extent can a non-linear situation be considered as a linear one?

4. Is it possible to identify all the constraints involved in tackling a problem by the linear programming method?

5. If we had attempted to solve the TV/armchair location problem in another way (i.e. other than by using linear programming), how effective would those solutions have been?

CHAPTER IX

Linear Programming - the Practice

AN APPLICATION OF LINEAR PROGRAMMING

Let us consider a company that produces and markets soup products, among others. It is not possible to make soup to order because (a) the raw materials used as ingredients are available seasonally, e.g. vegetables are not easily grown in winter although they may be frozen and stored at a cost, and (b) once the factory plant has been set to produce a particular variety of soup, the rate of canning is high and for reasons of economy large quantities are produced.

There is only one manufacturing plant and it is capable of producing each variety. Stocks of some lines have therefore to be built up in advance of requirement and there must be available at any given time at least as much stock as marketing have forecast will be sold before the next occasion when that particular line is produced.

Raw materials are frequently bought in bulk at discount rates. If they are bought in season they cost less than if bought out of season, but they are perishable and if only bought in season they would need to be kept in cold storage at a cost. On the other hand, if they are made up into finished goods, i.e. into cans of soup, there is a cost of holding large quantities of finished goods stock which may not be sold for some time. Such stock will need to be handled into storage, maintained in storage and handled out again when required. Handling charges can be high.

We may therefore ask whether it is more profitable to keep stock in the form of raw materials or finished goods.

A question posed in this way rather assumes that the transition from raw materials to finished goods is a minor consideration. This is not the case since there are production constraints such as a finite number of working hours, the time it takes to change plant over from working one variety of soup to another, and a minimum quantity that can be made in any one batch. If it is possible to work the plant three shifts, it is normally more costly on labour to run the third shift. The production constraints, therefore, introduce additional cost parameters and make the balance between stocking raw materials and finished goods that much more difficult.

We have discussed above some of the facts that need to be taken into account by the production planner at a soup-producing factory. With care and some simplification it is possible to write down the production planner's problem in the form of a linear programme, employing detailed costs of production, distribution and storage. The results of the L.P. would be information on which management could act. Over short periods of time, we would not expect marketing forecasts to be accurate, although we might expect them to lie within recognisable upper and lower limits. It is therefore very important that the company should have a contingency plan in case of an unexpected market surge, either upwards or downwards. The L.P. method is an excellent medium- to long-term planning tool, but difficulties may arise in the very short term when greater flexibility may be needed, combined with skilful management.

The "Mix" Problem

Problems which are suitable for analysis by the linear programming technique are frequently referred to as "mix" problems. For example, if it is required to produce a particular cattle food with predetermined characteristics of vitamins and proteins, it may be composed of a wide selection of ingredients, each contributing to the total of vitamins and proteins that are necessary. Each ingredient has a cost attached to it, and we simply wish to know which ingredients we should choose to satisfy the vitamin and protein needs, at minimum cost. By analysing and subsequently solving the problem in this way, we take little notice of what the cattle enjoy to eat, only what it costs to provide them with sufficient food to grow to the size we want them to be.

It is for this reason, the question of taste, that the linear programming technique has less applicability in the field of human food. It is extremely difficult, if not impossible, to devise a mathematical formula to describe taste, and to compile a formula which is linear is even more unlikely. In an affluent society, we humans can afford the luxury of choosing what we eat for reasons of taste, and any food producer who changes a winning recipe is likely to suffer in lost sales.

Oil refineries have similar problems to the cattle food manufacturer. They have raw materials from which they produce finished goods with precise characteristics and qualities. Crude oil is available from many places in the world, in varying quantities, at different prices, of a variety of qualities. They wish to produce petrol and other oil products at the lowest possible cost.

In the same vein, and to provide a worked example, a smelting company might wish to produce a blend of metal which has 40% lead and no more than 40% zinc. We shall assume that the blend may be obtained from four other possible blends, each with different constitutions and prices, as shown in Table V. The required blend is to be provided at minimum cost.

TABLE V: FOUR BLENDS OF METAL

Available blends	1	2	3	4	Required blend
% lead	30	50	50	60	40
% zinc	60	30	10	–	$\leqslant$ 40
% other metals	10	20	40	40	unrestricted
Cost/tonne	43	58	75	73	minimum

Numerical Solution (Simplex Method). Let y_1, y_2, y_3 and y_4 be the quantities of each available blend to be used in the required blend. Then $x_1 = y_1/(y_1 + y_2 + y_3 + y_4)$ is the fraction of available blend 1 to be used in the required blend. Similary for x_1, x_2 and x_4, therefore:

$$x_1 + x_2 + x_3 + x_4 = 1 \qquad (1)$$

Considering the lead requirement:

$$0.3_x y_1 + 0.5_x y_2 + 0.5_x y_3 + 0.6_x y_4$$
$$= 0.4 \ (y_1 + y_2 + y_3 + y_4)$$

that is:

$$0.3_x x_1 + 0.5_x x_2 + 0.5_{\ x} x_3 + 0.6_x x_4 = 0.4$$

or:

$$3x_1 + 5x_2 + 5x_3 + 6x_4 = 4 \qquad (2)$$

Considering the zinc requirement:

$$0.6_x y_1 + 0.3_x y_2 + 0.1_x y_3 \leqslant 0.4_x (y_1 + y_2 + y_3 + y_4)$$

that is:

$$0.6_x x_1 + 0.3_x x_2 + 0.1_x x_3 \leqslant 0.4$$

or:

$$6x_1 + 3x_2 + x_3 \leqslant 4 \qquad (3)$$

The x_1, x_2, x_3 and x_4 must all be greater than or equal to zero. We should like equation (3) to be an equality. To achieve that end, we recognise that since $6x_1 + 3x_2 + x_3$ is less than (or equal to) 4, it is in reality 4 less a non-negative quantity. Therefore, if we introduce a fifth unknown, x_5, which is itself greater than or equal to zero, we may rewrite the equation (3) as:

$$6x_1 + 3x_2 + x_3 + x_5 = 4 \qquad (4)$$

The cost of the required blend is:

$$43y_1 + 58y_2 + 75y_3 + 73y_4$$

which must be minimised by choosing values of y_1, y_2, y_3 and y_4, which also satisfy equations (1), (2) and (4).

By dividing this cost by $y_1 + y_2 + y_3 + y_4$, we can write the cost/tonne of the required blend as:

$$Z = 43x_1 + 58x_2 + 75x_3 + 73x_4 \qquad (5)$$

We have so far developed the following equations:

$$x_1 + x_2 + x_3 + x_4 = 1 \qquad (1)$$
$$3x_1 + 5x_2 + 5x_3 + 6x_4 = 4 \qquad (2)$$
$$6x_1 + 3x_2 + x_3 + x_5 = 4 \qquad (4)$$

and $Z = 43x_1 + 58x_3 + 75x_3 + 73x_4$ is to be minimised subject to the restrictions of equations (1), (2) and (4) and x_1, x_2, x_3, x_4 and x_5 all greater than or equal to zero.

We have three equations in five unknowns, so that if we were to put x_4 and x_5 equal to zero, we could find x_1, x_2 and x_3 explicitly. It so happens that the solutions for x_1, x_2 and x_3 are all greater than zero and therefore such a solution is a feasible one. In fact, we can rewrite equations (1), (2) and (4) as:

$$x_1 = \frac{1}{2} + \frac{x_4}{2} \qquad (6)$$

$$x_2 = \frac{1}{4} - \frac{3x_4}{4} - \frac{x_5}{2} \qquad (7)$$

$$x_3 = \frac{1}{4} - \frac{3x_4}{4} + \frac{x_5}{2} \qquad (8)$$

This is known as expressing the equations in canonical form, where the unknowns on the left-hand side, x_1, x_2 and x_3, do not appear on the right. We can choose to put $x_4 = x_5 = 0$, so a solution is therefore:

$$x_1 = \tfrac{1}{2}; x_2 = \tfrac{1}{4}; x_3 = \tfrac{1}{4}; x_4 = 0; x_5 = 0$$

x_1, x_2 and x_3 substituted into Z provide:

$$Z = 43(\tfrac{1}{2} + \tfrac{x_4}{2}) + 58(\tfrac{1}{4} - \tfrac{3x_4}{4} - \tfrac{x_5}{2}) + 75(\tfrac{1}{4} - \tfrac{3x_4}{4} + \tfrac{x_5}{2}) + 73\,x_4$$

which reduces to:

$$Z = 54\tfrac{3}{4} - 5\tfrac{1}{4}.\,x_4 + 8\tfrac{1}{2}.\,x_5$$

A cost/tonne of the required blend which can be achieved is therefore $54\tfrac{3}{4}$, but on inspecting the equation above for Z, it is clear that by increasing x_4, i.e. by making x_4 greater than zero, it is possible to reduce Z further. But an increase in x_4 increases x_1 in equation (6) and reduces x_2 and x_3 in equations (7) and (8) respectively.

The most we can increase x_4 is by $\tfrac{1}{2}$, which reduces both x_2 and x_3 to zero if we still maintain x_5 at zero. Either equation (7) or equation (8) will do, but we shall take equation (7) and put:

$$x_4 = \tfrac{1}{3} - \frac{4x_2}{3} - \frac{2x_5}{3} \qquad (9)$$

Substituting this value for x_4 into equations (6) and (8), we have:

$$x_1 = \tfrac{2}{3} - \frac{2x_2}{3} - \tfrac{1}{3}x_5 \qquad (10)$$

$$x_3 = 0 + x_2 + x_5 \qquad (11)$$

and in Z:

$$Z = 54\tfrac{3}{4} - 5\tfrac{1}{4}\left(\tfrac{1}{3} - \frac{4x_2}{3} - \frac{2x_5}{3}\right) + 8\tfrac{1}{2}x_5$$
$$= 53 + 7x_2 + 12x_5$$

An increase from zero of x_2 or x_5 will only increase Z, so the minimum value of Z subject to the original constraints of equations (1), (2) and (4) is 53.

The solution is to make up two-thirds of the required blend from available blend 1 and the remaining one-third from available blend 4. Blends 2 and 3 are not used.

Graphical Solution. We know that in equations (6), (7) and (8), x_1, x_2 and x_3 are each greater than or equal to zero. In which case:

$$\frac{x_4}{2} + \tfrac{1}{2} \geqslant 0$$

$$-\frac{3x_4}{4} - \frac{x_5}{2} + \tfrac{1}{4} \geqslant 0$$

$$-\frac{3x_4}{4} + \frac{x_5}{2} + \tfrac{1}{4} \geqslant 0$$

which can be represented graphically with x_4 and x_5 as axes, as shown in Fig. 10.

The area contained within the triangle formed by these three lines is the solution space, known as the "solution set", but there are additional restrictions. These are that x_4 and x_5 cannot be less than zero and so only the shaded area is applicable.

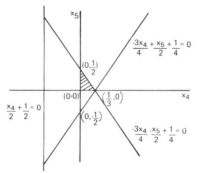

Fig. 10.   Graphical representation of the solution to a linear programming problem

The value of Z is $54\tfrac{3}{4} - 5\tfrac{1}{4}\, x_4 + 8\tfrac{1}{2}\, x_5$ and the family of lines of which this is a member is $-21x_4 + 34x_5 + C = 0$ where C can take any value. The line from this family which cuts the shaded space at its lowest point is the one which passes through $x_4 = \tfrac{1}{3}$ and $x_5 = 0$.

This is the required solution that, on substitution into the original equations yields $x_1 = \tfrac{2}{3}$; $x_2 = 0$; $x_3 = 0$; $x_4 = \tfrac{1}{2}$ and $x_5 = 0$ as before.

Transportation

Another common example of the application of linear programming is that known as transportation. It takes this name because it is generally associated with transport-type problems, although there are other problem areas to which it is applicable.

Imagine that a one-product manufacturer has three factories, each of which can supply any one of ten warehouses. The cost of carrying each unit of produce from each factory to each warehouse is known. Figure 11 illustrates this. Assume the cost from factory i to ware-

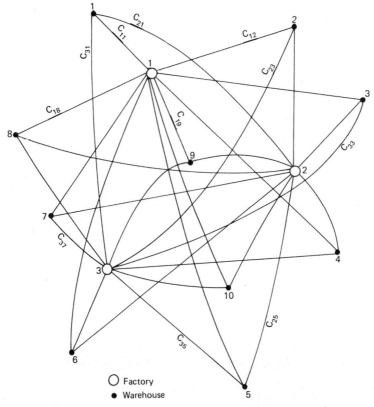

Fig. 11. A transportation problem

house j is C_{ij}. Let X_{ij} be the number of goods delivered from factory i to warehouse j. Then $X_{ij} \times C_{ij}$ is the cost of taking the goods from factory i to warehouse j. The sum of all these $X_{ij} \times C_{ij}$ terms is the total cost of supplying all the warehouses; and the objective is to minimise this quantity by choosing appropriate values of the X_{ij} and hence how much is sent from each factory to each warehouse.

This objective function is constrained by the quantities that are required at each warehouse, and which are available from each factory. We have it that the sum of the X_{ij} for each fixed i is a constant (factory constraint) and the sum of the X_{ij} for each fixed j is similarly constant (warehouse constraint).

The solution to this linear programming problem can be achieved by conventional means. However, because of the simpler format the problem takes (for example, none of the X_{ij} in the constraints equations is multiplied by a factor other than 1), a faster method of solution is possible.

SUMMARY

It will have been noted that each problem by linear programming described above consists of constraints and an objective function. Each of the constraints and the objective function can be represented in linear form. If this were not so, a solution could not be found. Unfortunately, relatively few problems can be described in such a way that they may be treated by the linear programming technique, but nevertheless, it still leaves a large number that can. It is often possible, with sufficient insight into the problem, to be able to approximate well enough to a linear formulation. Care must be taken, however, not to force the problem into a linear programming one just because it is possible to solve a problem so formed by the techniques we have discussed. There is no advantage to be gained by mathematical excellence if it is applied to the wrong problem. Equally, one should take care not to take into account all global influences, only those which truly matter.

DISCUSSION QUESTIONS

1. What are the real-life applications of linear programming? What are the shortcomings of this method of solution?

2. What do you think are the dangers of forcing a problem into linear form? To what extent might it be allowable?

3. Why is the linear programming technique particularly useful for "mix"-type problems?

4. Given two factories supplying three depots with one product, what are the factors to consider in determining how much should be delivered from each factory to each depot?

CHAPTER X

Dynamic Programming

THE APPLICATION OF DYNAMIC PROGRAMMING

The methods of dynamic programming were first formulated by Richard Bellman in his book of that name published in 1957.

Dynamic programming is a logical procedure by which a sequence of choices can be made, where each choice is between two or more possibilities. A common application of D.P. is in the field of replacement decisions. A car-hire company may wish to decide how frequently it should replace its vehicles, and how many. The frequency of replacement represents a sequence of decisions, and the number to be replaced represents the choice of possibilities of decision. A second example is the amount of goods (choice of possibilities) which a retailer might wish to order at intervals (sequence of choices).

If a problem can be broken down into a multi-stage decision process, for that is the process we have described above, then it is possible that a solution may be found by dynamic programming techniques. There may be many states (an infinite number even) or few, and at each stage there may be two, many or an infinite number of possible choices.

THE PRINCIPLE OF OPTIMALITY

In passing through the multi-stages of the decision, we are continuously seeking the optimum result. The method

Bellman provides to achieve this result depends upon his "Principle of Optimality" which may be stated in the following terms:

"An optimal policy has the property that whatever the initial state and initial decision are, the remaining decisions must constitute an optimal policy with regard to the state resulting from the first decision."

Applying the principle successively, whatever the point we have reached along the chain of stages of decision, if we assume that optimum decisions have been taken to reach the stage so far, all we now have to do is to make the optimum choice from those choices available to us at this present stage.

This is a relatively simple concept which we can reasonably accept without proof. The difficulty arises in formulating any given multi-stage decision problem so that it may be treated by dynamic programming methods and thus comply with the Principle of Optimality.

A Simple Optimal Path Problem

Suppose that we wish to move from one position A to another B. There are a variety of paths that we can take, but for simplicity we represent those paths as though they were on a grid system, as shown in Fig. 12. In fact, whatever the paths might be for the purposes of analysis, they could be laid out as though they were on a grid system, although probably less symmetrical than the example in Fig. 12.

The traveller can move only from left to right, and follows the diagonals. In mathematical terms, this means that he goes from position (i,j) either to position $(i+1, j+1)$ or to position $(i+1, j-1)$, and to no other.

Imagine that associated with each path is a penalty, which might be kilometres to be covered or perhaps toll charges. These penalties are shown in Fig. 12 for each path. The objective is to journey from A to B by those paths which incur the least total penalties.

It would be possible to consider every possible combin-

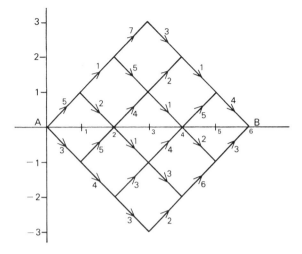

Fig. 12. A simple optimal path problem

ation of paths to reach the destination B, and from these choose the one which provides the minimum cost route. For a small problem, this is probably the sensible approach, but the larger the number of choices of paths, the greater the arithmetical task. However, by using the technique of dynamic programming it is possible to "home in" on the solution much more quickly.

We begin by recognising that the best, and only, route from position (5,1) suffers a penalty of 4. Similarly, the route from (5,-1) costs 3. To reach B from any position to the left of these points, the route must pass through one of these points. We are able therefore to apply the Principle of Optimality: from (5,1) and likewise from (5,-1) we know the optimal path and so we now need to determine the optimal paths from A to these positions.

To arrive at (5,1) or (5,-1) we must come from (4,2), (4,0) or (4,-2). From (4,2) to (5,1) costs 1, and it is impossible to reach (5,-1) from there (without breaking the rules). Similarly we can go only from (4,-2) to (5,-1), at a cost of 6. From (4,0) to B through (5,1) costs 5 + 4 = 9 and through (5,-1) costs 2 + 3 = 5. Clearly if we had

reached (4,0), the optimum route to B would be via
(5 -1) at a cost of 5.

We now move one stage nearer A and consider routes
from (3,3), (3,1), (3,-1) and (3,-3):

from (3,3) to B costs 3 + 1 + 4 = 8;

from (3,1) to B costs the minimum of $\begin{Bmatrix} 2 + 5 \\ 1 + 5 \end{Bmatrix} = 6$

i.e. from (3,1) to (4,2) costs 2, plus the 5 from (4,2) to
B we have calculated previously; similarly from (3,1) to
(4,0) costs 1, plus the 5 from (4,0) to B as above);

from (3,-1) to B costs the minimum of $\begin{Bmatrix} 4 + 5 \\ 3 + 9 \end{Bmatrix} = 9$

from (3,-3) to B costs 2 + 6 + 3 = 11

We may proceed in a similar way until we finally reach
A. The results of these calculations are shown in Fig. 13,
where the number at each intersection represents the minimum cost penalty to travel from the intersection to B.
The optimum path to take is shown as a heavy line.

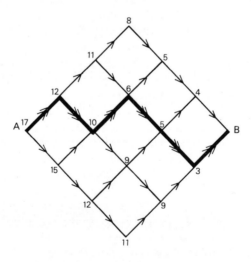

Fig. 13. The solution to the optimal path problem

The Allocation of Limited Resources

Suppose that we have a limited amount of one particular resource available, perhaps cash for investment or skilled workers. We have a number of tasks to which we might apply our resources (investment choices or jobs to be done) and we know what the return will be, given the amount of the resource that we allocate to each task.

Suppose that we have just five resource units available, and that we intend to allocate these units to three possible tasks:

If x units are allocated to task 1, the return is $30x - 5x^2$
If x units are allocated to task 2, the return is $9x$
If x units are allocated to task 3, the return is $40x - 8x^2$

The returns would normally represent some form of financial gain. We allocate x_1 to task 1, x_2 to task 2 and x_3 to task 3 so that $x_1 + x_2 + x_3 = 5$ and the total return, which we wish to maximise within that constraint, is $30x_1 - 5x_1^2 + 9x_2 + 40x_3 - 8x_3^2$.

Again, we could try all possible combinations and choose the one which gave the greatest return. In this particular case, there would be 21 such combinations. However, by using the principles of dynamic programming, we proceed as follows.

If we had just one task to perform, say task 1, we could apply all the resources (five units) to it and achieve a return of $30 \times 5 - 5 \times 5^2 = 25$. We might, however, wish to leave some units idle and so for each application of resources we have the corresponding returns, shown in Table VI (i).

We now bring task 2 into consideration. Table VI (ii) shows the returns for task 2 as well as those for task 1, for the equivalent number of resource units. If five units were available and we divided them in some way between task 1 and task 2, we would achieve a maximum return of 67 by allocating two units to task 1 and three units to task 2. By leaving one unit idle and limiting ourselves to only four units, we would apply two to each of the tasks, and

TABLE VI: THE ALLOCATION OF LIMITED RESOURCES

(i)

Resource units available	Return for task 1
0	0
1	25
2	40
3	45
4	40
5	25

(ii)

Resource units available	Return for task 1	Return for task 2
0	0	0
1	25	9
2	40	18
3	45	27
4	40	36
5	25	45

(iii)

Resource units available	Maximum returns from tasks 1 and 2	Units applied to task 1	Units applied to task 2
0	0	0	0
1	25	1	0
2	40	2	0
3	49	2	1
4	58	2	2
5	67	2	3

(iv)

Units applied to task 3	Return from task 3	Maximum returns from tasks 1 and 2	Total maximum return
5	0	0	0
4	32	25	57
3	48	40	88
2	48	49	97
1	32	58	90
0	0	67	67

obtain a maximum return of 58. Table VI *(iii)* shows the maximum returns and allocation of resources between the tasks for each level of resource availability.

The reason why we have allowed for idle resource units is so that when we introduce task 3 we can apply those "idle" units to that task. Since we know the best return we can achieve from each availability of resources on tasks 2 and 3, we can quickly determine what would be the total best return, including task 3 as well. We are again using the Principle of Optimality.

The allocation of nil resource units to task 3 provides nil return. Allocation of one, two, three, four and five resource units provide returns of 32, 48, 48, 32 and nil respectively. If no resource units are applied to task 3, then all five are applied to tasks 1 and 2, and we have seen that a maximum return of 67 is obtained from these two tasks by allocating two to task 1 and three to task 2. Arguing in the same way, if one resource unit is applied to task 3, that leaves four to be split between tasks 1 and 2, which yields the best result, a return of 58, by allocating two to each of them. The one unit with task 3 yields 32, so the best return is therefore 32 + 58 = 90. But next we must consider allocating two to task 3, and so on.

Table VI *(iv)* shows how the analysis develops, and the final result is that two units are employed on task 1, one unit on task 2 and two units on task 3, providing a maximum return of 40, 9 and 48 respectively, which makes a total of 97. The items underlined in Tables VI *(iii)* and *(iv)* identify this solution.

DISCUSSION QUESTIONS

1. What is dynamic programming?

2. To what kind of problems is dynamic programming applicable?

3. What is the Principle of Optimality?

4. Why should the dynamic programming technique be used?

5. If all the penalties above the x axis of Fig. 12 were increased by two, and those below the x axis were decreased by one, would the location of the optimum path change?

CHAPTER XI

The Theory of Games

DEFINITION OF A GAME

We each have, no doubt, a clear understanding of what we mean by a "game". It is basically a competitive activity between two or more players, or teams of players, who conform to predetermined rules, which state precisely how an eventual winner is to be decided.

It would be most satisfying if there could be developed a total theory of all possible games. Regrettably, this has not yet been achieved. Certainly computer programmes have been written to enable machines to play games such as draughts, and with particularly devastating effects. It is now possible for a computer, by means of a pseudo-learning process, to compete effectively at draughts with any human opponent, and to win. Clearly, a thorough understanding of the principles of the game of draughts has been developed. Unfortunately, analyses of the game of chess have been less successful, and no computer program yet exists which can compete effectively with even the chess player of moderate ability. Knowledge of other games is available to a greater or lesser degree.

In Operational Research terms, the "theory of games" applies to a very special kind of game, and to that kind only. It considers competition between two players, each of whom is able to choose just one of a pre-determined number of possible strategies. Each player makes his choice without any knowledge whatsoever of the choice that his opponent will make. Once the choices have been made, the gain or loss to each player is immediately identifiable.

Zero Sum Games

Table VII shows the possible outcomes of strategies which might be adopted by two players A and B. The strategies of A are represented as the rows of the matrix of Table VII and the strategies of B are the columns. If A were to choose strategy 3 and B were to choose strategy 2, the result of that round of the game would be the score shown in the third row and second column position of the matrix, i.e. the value 4.

TABLE VII: A ZERO SUM GAME

A \ B	1	2	3	4
1	12	3	8	2
2	6	3	6	10
3	5	4	7	5
4	9	2	10	16
5	8	1	1	13

The array of Table VII showing the results of related strategies is called the "gain matrix". The gain is always for player A. If, therefore, the result of the (3,2) strategy is a gain to A of 4, as we have seen, then there is a corresponding loss to B of 4. A minus figure shown in the gain matrix implies a loss to A and a gain to B.

These scoring rules mean that we are describing a "zero sum game". A gain to A is a loss to B and vice versa. The gain and loss when added together make zero, so we see that no greater rewards can be won from playing the game, only those which are already in the possession of A and B collectively. We might liken the situation to a game of cards between two players; each is trying to win money from the other and whatever strategies they each adopt, under no circumstances can they collectively gain from a third party.

If we were to take the part of A in playing the game of Table VII, we should need to adopt a particular strategy, without knowing before we adopt that strategy what action B might take. We are in the fortunate position of knowing before the event the outcomes of all possible strategy pairs. B is likewise in a similar position.

We make a fundamental assumption that the decisions B takes in choosing his strategies will be rational. He similarly makes the same assumption about us. That being so, we now proceed to select strategies which, over many playings of the game, should provide A with the highest average outcome.

It is important to note that the game is expected to be played many times, in fact to be really precise, an infinite number of times. If A and B were to choose their strategies just once, the outcome would depend entirely upon the degree of risk that each might be prepared to countenance, and would no longer depend upon rational thinking and decision-making.

Non-Zero Sum Games

A good example of a non-zero sum game is that known as the Prisoner's Dilemma.

Imagine two prisoners, A and B, each of whom is accused of jointly committing a crime, and each is in a separate police cell. They are told that if they both confess to the crime, each will receive an eight-year jail sentence. If neither confesses, evidence is so strong against them and the judge is likely to be so antagonised, that they will receive ten years in jail apiece. If however, one confesses and the other does not, the one who confesses will receive a fifteen-year jail sentence, and the one who does not confess will escape with a mere one-year sentence. Clearly, the decision to confess or not confess depends entirely on what decision the other party takes. Yet the police ensure that there is no means of communication.

There is no straightforward solution to this dilemma

(other than perhaps remaining honest citizens in the first place), but it does illustrate an example of a non-zero sum game.

Deciding Between Alternatives

We have so far discussed the rules of the game of Table VII in general terms and we must now be more mathematically explicit. There are two basic attitudes which we may adopt to decide between alternatives. These are:
1. To minimise loss;
2. To maximise gain, or possible outcome.
   Another way of expressing these attitudes is:
1. To minimise regret (if objective is not achieved);
2. To maximise security of achieving objective.

Normally, between these extremes there is a continuum of expected or hoped-for outcomes. With the rules of the theory of games however, we shall remain strictly with these objectives.

COMPETITIVE ACTIVITY

Let us now consider a simplified practical example. Let us suppose that firm A, in deciding its advertising strategy, really has just two alternatives. Either it advertises on television or in the national press. Firm B, the only other competitor in the field, can equally decide to advertise on television or in the press; from past experience, no other advertising medium has as great an effect on the product as do these two.

Firms A and B are both anxious to improve market share. The market is, however, a static one and the effect of one company achieving an increase in market share is to reduce that of the other by an equal amount. It has been learnt in the past that if both companies advertise on the same medium at the same time, firm A always gains two per cent of the market share from television and one per cent from the press. It is as if firm B makes the customers

aware of the product but not of B's name, and as A is
the market leader of the two they buy A's products.
On the other hand, if they advertise on different media,
B on television gains a two per cent increase in share but
B in the newspapers simply counteracts A on television.
These advertising strategies can be sufficiently well isolated
from other activities in the company to make the
conclusions reasonable ones and valid. Both A and B are
frequently advertising in these ways and they have canvass
periods which tend to coincide, thus causing their
advertising to occur at very nearly the same times and at
the same intensities. Besides, if one advertised and the
other did not, the advertising firm would increase its
market share by at least ten per cent.

TABLE VIII: A ZERO SUM GAME : MARKET SHARE

		B	
		TV	NP
A	TV	2	0
	NP	- 2	1

Results for A

From the information given, we can compile Table VIII
above, showing the effect on the market share of A.
Reading across the rows of the table, we see that if A
advertises on TV and B advertises on TV, the gain to A is
2 per cent. If however B advertises in the newspapers, NP,
the gain to A is zero. Similarly for the second row, if A
advertises in NP and B on TV, A loses 2 per cent, but if
they both advertise in NP, A gains 1 per cent. The
question now remains, which is the best strategy for A to
adopt to counteract B, not knowing in advance what B
will do? We can solve the problem with the aid of the
diagram in Fig. 14. The left-hand vertical line measures
the gain to A if it chooses NP. The right-hand line
measures the gain from TV. Line *P* illustrates the effect of
B choosing NP and line *Q* shows B choosing TV. The
point of intersection of *P* and *Q* divides each of *P* and *Q* in

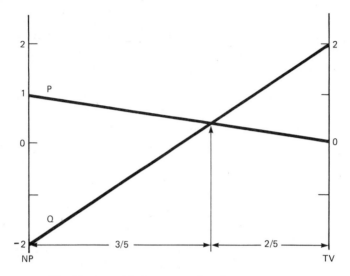

Fig. 14. A graphical representation of a zero sum game

the ratio 3 to 2 which tells us how often A should use TV (and hence how often it should use NP). Assuming that the probability of B going for one or the other is the same, i.e. 50 per cent, we can deduce that on three occasions out of every five A should advertise on TV.

Dominant Strategies

It is sometimes appropriate for a player to choose just one strategy from a selection of strategies, and to keep solely to that strategy. This is called the "dominant" strategy.

TABLE IX: A GAIN MATRIX SHOWING
DOMINANT STRATEGIES

Players A	B	1	2	3
1		-4	-2	5
2		3	-1	2
3		6	-4	-2

Consider the gain matrix in Table IX. From player B's standpoint, column 2 is always a better choice than column 3: it ensures that the gain to A is lower, whatever choice A makes. Since both A and B are assumed to take rational decisions, A realises that B will always prefer column 2. He therefore excludes column 3 from consideration.

It follows that row 2 is more sensible than row 3 because the return to A is always greater (we have excluded column 3). The matrix is now reduced to rows 2 and 3 and columns 1 and 2. At this stage it is clear that B will still choose column 2. In column 2, A chooses row 2. This means that A will always choose row 2 and B will choose column 2. The result of the game is that A will receive -1 (or B receives +1).

As rational players, both A and B, no matter how many trials they conduct, will always keep to the same choice of strategy. If A makes any other choice, the gain could be less (or the loss more). If B chooses another strategy, A may gain more (or lose less). B minimises his potential regret, whilst A maximises his potential security.

Saddle Points

To the gain matrix shown in Table X has been added a column which lists the minima of the rows. The additional row shows the maxima of the columns.

TABLE X. A GAIN MATRIX SHOWING SADDLE POINTS

Players A \ B	1	2	3	4	Row Minima
1	12	3	0	2	0
2	0	3	6	10	0
3	5	4	7	5	4
4	9	2	0	16	0
5	8	1	1	13	1
Column Maxima	12	4	7	16	

A would wish to choose his strategy so that his return is a maximum, if A knew in advance (which A does not, according to the rules) what strategy B would adopt. A's objective therefore is to achieve a solution from the "column maxima" row. Likewise, B wishes to choose his strategy so that A's return is a minimum (without knowing in advance what A will do) and therefore hopes for a solution from the "row minima" column.

If A were to choose just one strategy, he would prefer row 4 in the hope of gaining 16, but knows that B would not allow him to do so (B would be expected to choose column 3). If however A chooses row 3, it is apparent that B would choose column 2 because B could ensure that A would gain the least as a result of the row 3 strategy. Yet given a choice of column 2 by B, A would choose row 3 because it maximises A's return.

It follows that because the maximum of the row minima coincides with the minimum of the column maxima, that is the result of the game, and the necessary strategies of both A and B (assuming rational behaviour).

Mixed Strategies

We have already discussed an example of mixed strategy in considering the market share example of Table VIII. Dominance and saddle points, if they exist, identify strategies where both A and B choose, continuously, just one strategy, known as a "pure strategy". Mixed strategies mean that for some of the time one strategy is used and at other times other strategies are used.

The objective of game theory is to determine the frequency with which each strategy should be applied. The strategies are adopted at random (i.e. without allowing the opponent to identify a pattern), so that over very many plays of the game, the expected or average result is that which the game theory has calculated, given the particular choice of mixed strategy.

DISCUSSION QUESTIONS

1. How does the Operational Research definition of a game differ from the more usual definition?

2. What assumption do we make about the players?

3. What is the difference between a zero sum game and a non-zero sum game?

4. What objectives do we have when deciding between alternatives?

5. If the theory of games were to be applied to an advertising strategy decision, what facts would it be necessary to collect?

6. By applying dominance and then saddle points to Table VII, determine the result of the game.

CHAPTER XII

Network Analysis

SCOPE OF NETWORK ANALYSIS

It is usual to think of network analysis as a procedure for scheduling and controlling work. Many problems, however, may be represented as a collection of inter-connected linkages. We might, for example, consider the optimum route that a salesman should take if he is to call on a number of customers in different towns in such a way that he minimises total journey time, or distance covered. Such a requirement is known as the "travelling salesman problem" and in diagrammatic form is represented as a number of separate points which are inter-connected to all others, with an optimum route super-imposed upon them.

Another kind of network problem is that known as "vehicle scheduling". Here we have a central depot which is to deliver goods to a number of outlying stations. A fleet of vehicles is available at the depot and the question is to determine which selection of customers should each vehicle visit, and in which order, to minimise the total distance covered by the whole fleet.

We might consider the problem one stage further back and discuss how best to site the depot in the first place. It is usual for the customers to be known and already specifically located, and for there to be an awareness of the projected off-take of goods by each customer. This being so, if we simplify the situation (no doubt too much to be reasonably practical, but to stand as an illustration only), and assume that deliveries can be made directly as the crow flies from wherever the depot is to be sited, there is a particularly easy and non-mathematical way of choosing the site. If each customer is assumed to carry a weight, equivalent on some appropriate scale to the amount of goods that he requires to be delivered from the depot, the optimum siting for the depot depends upon the influence of those weights, each upon the other. A simple way of determining that influence is to take a map of the area in which the customers are situated, to make holes through the map where each customer is placed (it would be advisable to use a map pasted on to a hard backing!), to associate weights as described above to each customer and to tie those weights to pieces of string which pass through the respective hole in the map and join together in one place on the top side of the map. The weights hang down beneath. The position at which the join of all pieces of string rests in equilibrium is the site location for the depot. Here is an example of Operational Research in action without mathematical analysis, although it must be admitted that to justify the location so found as the optimum siting requires mathematical proof (and a resting place that does not coincide with a mountain peak or a lake!).

CRITICAL PATH PLANNING

Perhaps the most commonly accepted application of network analysis is in the field known as critical path planning. C.P.P., as it is known, is really an extension of the ideas of Gantt charts. Any construction work or other similar operation consists of a large number of sub-tasks. If those tasks are arranged in a logical fashion, some in sequence and others in parallel, the total job will be completed faster, probably more cheaply and certainly more efficiently.

Firstly all sub-tasks must be identified. Although apparently a statement of the obvious, it is often the need to identify the sub-tasks in a formal way that uncovers potential trouble spots, allows corrective action to be taken and provides the greatest benefit. Associated with each sub-task, which we shall now call by the more usual name of "activity", is a duration of time over which the activity is due to last. The start of an activity and the end of an activity are known as events. Since some activities precede others, the event which is the end of one activity is also the start of any activity which immediately succeeds it, and which is dependent upon the completion of the preceding activity before it may begin.

In critical path planning we are concerned with the order in which activities take place, as well as their time duration. Diagrammatically, the line which represents the activity is not drawn of a length equivalent to the time duration of the activity, as it is with the Gantt chart.

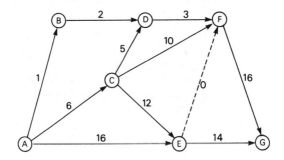

Fig. 15. A conceptual network, showing critical path planning

Figure 15 illustrates a conceptual network, showing activities in sequence and those which may run in parallel. Where more than one activity emerges from one event, not one of those activities may commence until the end of all preceding activities entering that event has been reached.

Events are identified as circles, designated by the capital letters A to G. Activities are those lines which join events. The time duration of each activity is shown in the figure. The dotted line activity E to F has a time duration of zero, and this is the conventional way of showing an activity with zero time duration. It is known as a dummy activity and is there simply to ensure that activity F to G does not begin until those which end at E are fully completed. Activities which end at event F must likewise be completed before activity F to G may commence.

Event A is at the start of the activities and event G is at the finish. It is evident that event B cannot occur until at least one time period has elapsed; likewise C cannot occur until at least six time periods have elapsed and E must wait for at least sixteen. Event D cannot take place until both A to B to D has occurred and A to C to D. The former takes 1 + 2 = 3 time periods, the latter 6 + 5 = 11 time periods. Event D must wait at least eleven time periods, therefore, before it can take effect.

By a similar argument we can show that event E will not be fully satisfied until at least eighteen time periods have elapsed. Carrying these calculations through to the final event G, we find that the earliest time that the whole project can be completed is at time period 34. We now tabulate the earliest occurrence of each of the events as follows:

TABLE XI: ANALYSIS OF A PROJECT
BY NETWORK ANALYSIS

Event	Earliest Occurrence
A	Zero
B	1
C	6
D	11
E	18
F	18
G	34

The earliest occurrence of the project, which we also have called previously the earliest completion, is at 34 time periods. This also represents the total time that the project will take if it is to be conducted in the most efficient way.

The Critical Path. Working backwards from G, we can see that F must have occurred by time period 18, otherwise G will not be reached by time period 34 (i.e. 34 - 16 = 18). Taking the direct path from E to G, we see that E must have taken place by time period 20. But considering that E precedes F which in turn precedes G, E is also constrained by the E to F to G route which takes 0 + 16 = 16 time periods. From that direction, E must have been completed by time period 18. Given that the latest occurrence of F is at time period 18, it means that the latest occurrence of D must be 15 (18 - 3 = 15). Event C is the starting point for three activities, of which the most critical is activity C to E. It will be seen that C must have occurred by time period 6 to enable E to be reached by time period 18. If C is satisfied by time period 6, then F can be reached by time period 18 with two to spare, and likewise D will have a reserve of four time periods.

Table XII below incorporates the new latest occurrence times we have calculated.

TABLE XII: FURTHER ANALYSIS OF A PROJECT BY NETWORK ANALYSIS

Event	Earliest Occurrence	Latest Occurrence
A	0	0
B	1	13
C	6	6
D	11	15
E	18	18
F	18	18
G	34	34

The above table identifies those events which cannot afford to suffer delay: any delay in those events will mean that the full project will not be completed in the minimum time of 34 time periods. The events to which we refer are those for which the earliest occurrence is the same as the latest occurrence: they are events A, C, E, F, and G.

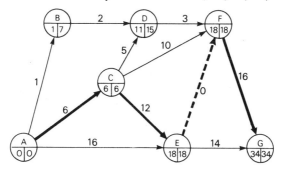

Fig. 16. The critical path of the network

Figure 16 highlights these events by showing the activities which join them as heavier lines. It will be seen that these activities are the most critical ones because any delay in these activities will delay the whole project. They are said to lie on the "critical path" of the network. The numbers, which have been inserted in the circles that represent the events of the network, are on the left, the earliest occurrence, and on the right, the latest occurrence of each respective event. The difference between these two numbers represents the amount of delay or "slack" as it is called, which the preceding activities may enjoy without delaying the project as a whole.

New Product Launch

Critical path planning has proved itself to be invaluable to the construction industry and was, for example, used extensively in planning the Victoria Underground line in London. It can be just as useful, however, for the smaller job, and preparing the lunch or making a pot of tea or coffee might be completed a little more efficiently if the sequence of tasks were firstly drawn out as a critical path diagram. Let us, however, consider just one practical example of critical path planning.

Suppose that a food company is considering the introduction of a new line into its product range. There are several stages of development which have to be considered, many of which may overlap. The sooner the new product is launched, the quicker will be the return on the capital spent in developing the product, and the less time there will be for competition to prepare for its own similar launch. Management therefore have two principal objectives; first to set the product on the market as soon as possible and second to do so within a predetermined budget. Some of the work which needs to be carried out before the new product can be put on the market is listed below.

1. There must be sufficient research to determine whether or not the product is feasible.
2. A decision must be taken whether it is worth developing further.
3. Research must be continued to find the best ingredients, method of continuous production, etc.
4. Manufacturing plant must be designed, ordered and installed.
5. A suitable and reliable supply of raw materials must be found.
6. Advertising strategy must be agreed and trial markets found.
7. The sales force must be trained and administrative procedures drawn up.

Clearly there is considerable work to be done before the product reaches the consumer.

The sequence of work leading up to the new product launch can dramatically affect the date of completion. Several tasks can be overlapped and it is important that this be done, provided the resources for each job are available. For example, it may be that clerical staff are required for two separate jobs, but there are an insufficient number of clerks. Two such jobs cannot be run together. The diagram shown in Fig. 17 illustrates a possible sequence for the work. It can be seen that certain jobs,

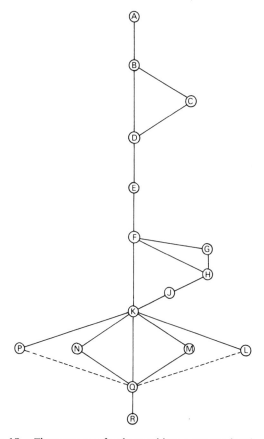

Fig. 17. The sequence of tasks to achieve a new product launch

AB Basic research on product feasibility
BD Market research
BC Product research
CD Plant design for trial quantities
DE Product costings
EF Decide upon trial
FH Order raw materials
FG Order plant
FK Design advertising schemes
GH Install plant
HJ Run local trials
JK Decide whether to go national

KM Order more plant
KP Order raw materials
KL Train sales force
KQ Prepare documentation
KN Choose advertising medium
NQ Design packaging
MQ Install plant
QR Launch product
LQ/

PQ Dummy tasks, i.e. tasks with no duration, used only to define the order in which jobs should take place from the standpoint of logic, can take place at the same time. There may be, however, resource constraints which prevent this from being so in practice, as, for example, the clerks mentioned above. The time that a job takes to complete depends to some extent on the resources that are applied to it. If expected job durations and available resources are allocated to each job, it is possible to identify that sequence of events which takes the longest time, and hence those jobs which are the critical ones. Resources applied to jobs that are not critical would be better used on the critical ones to reduce the overall time, although such redeployment of resources would only be made up to the point at which the non-critical job is made to be critical.

Resources are most likely to be labour and plant, but cash too can be considered as a resource. As a generalisation, the more labour and plant we use, the shorter the time an individual job takes and the more it costs. The objective is to balance time, costs and other resources such that the new product can be put on the market with a significant lead on competition but at a cost which provides an acceptable profit.

Resource Allocation

We have seen in the example of the new product launch that the time an activity takes is dependent upon the resources allocated to it. The times are, of course, estimates of the duration of each activity and are usually based upon resources known to be available. Once the critical path is identified, it becomes evident (unless the scheduler is particularly fortunate) that certain resources could be better deployed elsewhere to either speed up the project, or smooth out the demand for total resources.

If little attention is paid to resource allocation at the planning stages, it is likely that resources will be required in peaks and troughs. Unless the employer is prepared to adopt a policy of hire and fire, he will want his labour resources, for example, to be set at a constant level.

It is the function of resource allocation methods to achieve this smoothing and to highlight when resources should be transferred from one activity to another to achieve a less costly and more efficient total operation. The approach is usually to employ the services of a computer, for which several programs have been written for resource allocation. The computer is used to carry out the tedious arithmetic whilst the scheduler with the aid of the critical path planning techniques already discussed analyses and produces approved resource allocation solutions.

PERT

PERT stands for "project evaluation and review technique". It is basically the same as the critical path planning method we have so far discussed but it attempts to pay greater attention to estimating the duration of each activity. These time estimates are doubtless the most critical and sensitive part of the whole critical path planning methodology. If the time estimates are wrong, conclusions drawn about the total length of the project and the identification of the critical path are of limited value.

PERT was first developed by the U.S. Navy in the early '60s. The idea is that whoever is responsible for making the time estimates for each activity should provide not just one figure (i.e. that person's best estimate), but three such estimates. These three figures are his most optimistic, his most pessimistic, and his most likely estimate. Some kind of weighting is then applied to these three figures (for example, 3 x pessimistic plus 4 x the most likely plus 3 x the optimistic, all divided by 10), and the resultant figure is treated as the estimate which is then used for the purposes of the critical path planning, as before. Because weights have been applied in this way, it is possible to assume that we have a distribution of estimates for each activity, a distribution in the sense that we have discussed in the chapters on Statistics. From these distributions we can deduce a crude measure of standard deviation. As a result, not only can we identify the critical path of the total project based on the durations calculated from the original three estimates, but we can also determine the range in which the true total project time will lie, within statistical confidence limits, by taking due account of the standard deviations.

The principal advantage claimed for PERT is that the time estimates for the durations of the activities will be more accurate, within a range. This may be so, but from a practical standpoint, it is probably even more difficult to obtain three estimates from the individuals responsible for each activity, than it is to obtain just one estimate. Furthermore, if estimates must be obtained from several individuals responsible for groups of activities of the project, there remains the danger that each will base his estimates on different premises. Taking three estimates per activity might simply mean several additional and different assumptions on which the estimates are based.

DISCUSSION QUESTIONS

1. What kind of problems lend themselves to solution by network analysis?

2. What is critical path planning and why is it so called?

3. In Fig. 15, if the time durations of activities AC and CF remain the same, but those above these two activities are increased by three and those below are increased by one, does the critical path change?

4. Why use critical path planning?

5. What action can be taken to speed up a total project?

6. Are there any advantages in using PERT?

CHAPTER XIII

Replacement Theory

THE NEED TO REPLACE

Most items we purchase need to be replaced at some time in their lives. Either they fail completely, deteriorate to such an extent that they no longer perform the function for which they were designed, or they become obsolete. Examples of these three categories are:

1. Failure — light bulbs, some engine parts;
2. Deterioration — vehicle tyres, machine cutting-tools; and
3. Obsolescence — plant and equipment in a factory which has become outmoded and relatively inefficient due to technical innovations.

It might be said that the need to replace arises only when the useful life of the item under consideration for replacement has come to an end (i.e. has failed, has reached a point at which further deterioration cannot be tolerated, or is recognisably so inefficient compared with other items now on the market, which can do the same job, that it must be replaced). If this were so, the decision "when to replace" would be a simple and obvious one to take. In the domestic situation, we replace electric light bulbs after they have failed because (a) the inconvenience of not having sufficient light during the time between failure and replacement is tolerable, and (b) there is no cost involved in actually making the replacement.

In the factory or business situation, however, the cost of

failure is often appreciably higher than the cost of the item itself that has failed. For example, many components used in navigational equipment are expensive in themselves but failures of these components while in active service may lead to outcomes that are very costly. In the field of aviation, one would not wish to wait until a particular part of an aircraft fractured, which might result in the loss of human life as well as financial cost. One would instead carry out preventive maintenance and therefore replace components in anticipation of failure.

In industrial equipment, a failure may lead to loss of production and perhaps damaged output. We must consider therefore three kinds of cost:

1. The cost of the item itself;
2. The cost of the effect of the failure; and
3. The cost involved in actually replacing the item.

The last cost would include labour and fuel costs. Take for example the replacement of light bulbs for street lighting. If they were replaced simply whenever a light bulb failed, a maintenance man would be sent on each occasion and by far the greater part of his cost would be travelling to and from the offending lamp standard, rather than making the actual replacement itself. It follows that the greater the number of failures occurring at one time, the cheaper it is to replace them as a whole.

A possible way in which we might reduce the costs associated with sudden failure is to predict when those failures are likely to occur and to replace components before they actually do fail. It is unlikely that we would be able to predict accurately when components would fail and therefore this approach has limited application. Nevertheless, regular inspection of components can lead to useful predictions of times of failure. The problem would then be to decide when inspections should be made. We might avoid that difficulty if we know instead the life or probability distribution of the age at which failure occurs. For example, we might know from quality control tests at the manufacturing source that for any batch of fluorescent tubes made at the same time, ten per cent of them fail in the first year, twenty per cent in the second year, thirty per cent in the third, and forty per cent in the fourth. If this were so, we would be sure that no fluorescent tube would last longer than four years. The probability of failure in this particular example is dependent upon age; the older the tube the greater the chance that it will fail.

REPLACEMENT DUE TO FAILURE

Replacement of a Single Component

Let us now consider the situation in which we have one component and we wish to decide whether it should be replaced only at the moment that it fails, or at planned time intervals and between those intervals as well if it should fail in the meantime. In effect, we wish to determine whether planned replacement should be used, and if so, at what age of the component.

We shall consider an installation that consists of a single component (and we shall take a conveyor belt as the example) which is subject to failure. The component operates in discrete cycles (for the conveyor belt, shifts) and it is not possible to say before-hand in which cycle the component will fail. To simplify the discussion, we shall imagine that the system will operate for an unlimited number of cycles (or shifts) in the future and so the measure by which we shall decide the optimum solution will be the expected cost of operation of the component per cycle. Our objective will be to minimise the expected cost per cycle.

Figure 18 illustrates a planned replacement strategy. Replacement occurs either on failure or, in this particular example, after six cycles of operation. Instead of restricting ourselves to planned replacement after six cycles of operation, we shall attempt to devise a general

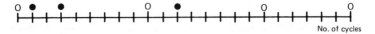

Planned replacement after T cycles of operation

T = 6   ● Failure   O Planned replacement

Fig. 18.   A replacement strategy for a single item

formula which provides us with a total minimum cost operation by assuming that the planned replacement occurs after T cycles.

To do this, we must first consider the expected number of components that will be used over a very large number of cycles, which we shall call N. The components used will consist of those which have been replaced because they have failed, and those which have been replaced because their useful life of T cycles has expired.

Since we know the probable life expectancy of the components, we can calculate the average life of a component. To illustrate, consider the fluorescent tubes we discussed previously. We said that ten per cent lasted for one year, twenty per cent for two years, thirty per cent for three years and forty per cent for four years. The average life is therefore:

$$1/10 \times 1 + 2/10 \times 2 + 3/10 \times 3 + 4/10 \times 4 = 3 \text{ years}$$

If in general we say that the average life of a component is $L(T)$ then it follows that the number of components that we would expect to use in N cycles would be $N/L(T)$. We now have to consider the number of components that will have failed within the life span of T cycles and the number of components that will still be functioning when they are replaced (i.e. will have lasted T cycles). If $P(T)$ is the probability that a component will not have failed within the T cycles (in the fluorescent-tube example the probability that a tube will last longer than two years is 0.7) then $1 - P(T)$ is the probability that a component will fail within the first T cycles of its life. The expected number of replacements in N cycles due to failure is therefore:

$$\frac{N \times (1 - P(T))}{L\,(T)}$$

and the expected number of planned replacements in N cycles is:

$$\frac{N \times P(T)}{L\,(T)}$$

If we now represent the cost of replacing one failed component by C_F (this cost to include not only the cost of the component itself but also the cost of the labour to carry out the replacement and any lost production due to the failure) and the cost of planned replacement as C_R (which will presumably be a lower cost than C_F because no lost production would have occurred), then it can be shown that the expected total cost over the N cycles is equal to:

$$\frac{N \times (1 - P(T)) \times C_F}{L(T)} + \frac{N \times P(T) \times C_R}{L(T)}$$

It follows therefore that the expected cost per cycle with planned replacement after T cycles is $C_F - (C_F - C_R) \times P(T)$ all divided by $L\,(T)$.

It should be noted that preventive replacement cannot always be justified, as for example when the conditional probability of failure is independent of age. This would be the case if failure were due to random causes such as shocks or accidents.

Group Replacement

We shall now consider a system that contains a large group of identical low-cost items for which the probability of individual failure increases the older the item becomes. The cost of replacing these items is the same no matter how many are replaced at one time. This means that in deciding the least-cost replacement strategy we must look very closely at replacing all items in the group simultaneously at fixed intervals of time. Irrespective of when an individual item had previously failed, it would still be replaced when the time came to effect the group replacement policy. Unlike the previous discussion of single component replacement, under group replacement it is not necessary to keep records of the ages of individual components. Perhaps the most common example of this type of policy is that which concerns the replacing of street-light bulbs where the major cost of replacement is that of bringing a vehicle and men to replace the defective bulbs.

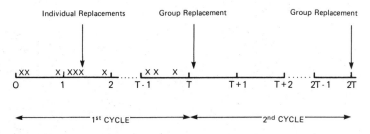

Fig. 19. A group replacement strategy

Figure 19 provides a diagrammatic representation of the group replacement strategy. It assumes that group replacement occurs after a fixed interval of time T (days, weeks, hours). As we have already discussed in the previous section, there are means by which we can identify the average life of an item, which we shall denote by L. If there are G items in the total group, then G/L is the average number of replacements after failure per time period. If C_I is the cost of individually replacing an item (which includes the cost of the item plus the replacement cost which we have said is the same irrespective of the number replaced) then the average, or expected, cost per time period is $G \times C_I/L$.

This simple formula takes no account of group replacement. We wish to see, therefore, whether group replacement will reduce the total costs that will be incurred by replacing a failed item only when it is necessary to do so.

We must now consider two types of cost: the cost of replacing all items at one time and the cost of replacing the individual items as they fail between each group replacement or cycle. The expected total cost per cycle consists, therefore, of two elements: the cost of replacing the items as a group, which we denote as C, plus the cost of replacing each individual item (C_I) multiplied by the expected number of individual replacements during the cycle. This latter number requires some mathematical manipulation since we must take into account the fact that if a failed item is replaced some time after group replacement and before the next, the probability of it failing again is different from that which would have been the probability if the original item had not failed. We shall simply denote the expected number of individual replacements during the cycle as E, in which case, bearing in mind that planned group replacement occurs every T periods, the expected cost per period is:

$$C/T + C_I \times E/T$$

It will be seen that different group replacement costs will arise depending upon the interval, T, between group replacements. It so happens that if a plot is made of Cost against Interval, one of the two graphs in Fig. 20 will

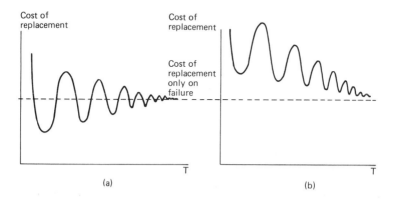

Fig. 20. Graph of group replacement costs against time

apply. In both cases, as the interval T becomes long, they converge to the dotted line which is shown. This line represents the expected cost which obtains if items are replaced only upon failure. If the first graph is a representation of the replacement strategy under consideration, then clearly group replacement, at intervals of T, provide the minimum cost answer. For the second graph, group replacement is not appropriate.

DETERIORATION AND OBSOLESCENCE

Replacement due to Deterioration

To illustrate this kind of replacement, we consider the problem faced by an engineering company in deciding when to renew or regrind its cutting tools.

There are two opposing costs which must be taken into account. On the one hand, the faster the machines are set to run, the more goods they produce and the greater the profit potential for the company. But on the other hand, fast operating machines wear out that much more quickly.

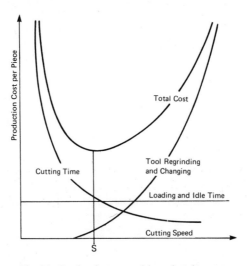

Fig. 21. Production cost with tool replacement

Figure 21 shows the relationship between these two costs. As cutting speed increases, so the production cost per item reduces. But at higher speeds, tool replacements are required more frequently and so these costs experience a corresponding increase.

The sum of these two costs provides the total cost, of which there is an obvious minimum cost point, represented in Fig. 21 by the cutting speed S. If minimum production cost per item is the objective of management, then the cutting tools should be set to run at speed S. However, if other criteria are of greater importance, for example the need to produce a large quantity by a given deadline, then choosing the obvious minimum cost point is not appropriate. Because there exists, therefore, a reason to produce more, there is also a cost benefit. If this benefit is considered in the total cost curve, it will shift the minimum cost point to a cutting speed at a higher level.

We have not discussed the formulation of the curves in Fig. 21. They would need to be analysed in detail, in a similar way to the formula that we developed for single component replacement, as well as for group replacement.

Replacement due to Obsoloescence

Obsolescence implies that a piece of equipment or plant is working less efficiently than a replacement might. In considering what action to take when obsolescence becomes apparent, it is important to avoid being influenced by production records from the past. An analysis of future expected performance of present equipment, in terms of cost, must be carried out as well as an assessment of the costs involved if replacement equipment were purchased, installed, operated and maintained. These two separate categories of costs must then be compared and a decision taken whether to retain present equipment, or replace with new.

The difficulty is that in general the cost figures are often difficult to compare because they span different time periods, although it is possible for it to be obvious that replacement is better than continuing with machinery which has become obsolete. If it is not obvious, a proper comparison may be made by considering the two alternatives as investments. By applying discounted cash flow methods, discussed in the next chapter, a rational choice may be made.

DISCUSSION QUESTIONS

1. When do we need to consider replacement and for what reasons?

2. What factors do we need to take into account?

3. Why is it sometimes better to replace items as a group instead of simply replacing whenever an item fails?

4. What data is necessary before a replacement strategy can be determined?

5. What are the practical applications of replacement theory?

CHAPTER XIV

Return on Investment

INVESTMENT CHOICE

Investment is a commitment of resources made in the hope of realising benefits that are expected to accrue over a reasonably long future period of time. In this chapter we shall confine ourselves totally to money investments, but there are various other kinds. Gifts, in one form or another, might be made for services rendered, or in anticipation of future services expected from the recipient. We expect to reap a fruitful harvest in the autumn from seeds sown in the spring. The advantage to be gained from restricting ourselves to a discussion of money investment, however, is that both the capital sum laid out in the first place and the subsequent return on that investment, can be measured in a quantifiable way, and on a common scale.

Anyone who has a sum of money he wants to invest in anticipation of a reward, has a number of choices in front of him. But it is only with National Savings Certificates, building society saving schemes, bank deposits and the like that investors will know precisely (perhaps we should say "almost precisely") what rate of interest he will earn and therefore the yield from his investment. When it comes to considering other purchases, such as company shares, commodities, oil paintings or property, the return from the investment is by no means as clear cut, or even certain. But even if it were possible to say exactly how much the return on the investment would be, and when, it would not be a simple decision to choose the optimum. We should have immediate difficulty in what we mean by optimum, as Table XIII illustrates. It is assumed that the investment, or outlay, is made at the beginning of the first year and that proceeds are received at the end of each year in a lump sum.

TABLE XIII: RETURN ON INVESTMENT

Investment	Initial cost (£)	Net cash proceeds per year		
		Year 1	Year 2	Year 3
A	10,000	10,000		*
B	10,000	5,000	5,000	5,000
C	10,000	2,000	4,000	12,000
D	10,000	10,000	3,000	3,000
E	10,000	6,000	4,000	5,000
F	10,000	8,000	8,000	2,000

Ranking by Inspection

This method of choice has very limited use, but it does enable obviously inferior investments to be rejected. It is clear that investment D is better than A since, although they each yield £10,000 in the first year, D provides £3,000 in each of the two succeeding years, after A has finished. E looks better than B because the total proceeds up to any point for E are as great if not greater than those for B. A similar argument might be applied to F and C.

The difficulty arises when trying to decide between D, E and F. It is here that we need to be far more specific about what we expect to gain from the initial investment. Although it would appear at this stage that we have rejected A, B and C in favour of D, E and F (i.e. D or E or F will always seem to be preferred to A or B or C respectively), we shall find that as we define our optimum investment criteria more closely, D, E or F do not naturally turn out to be the best investments.

Pay-Back Period

This method of investment analysis is very simple to apply and very popular. The "pay-back period" is defined as the length of time required for a stream of cash proceeds produced by an investment to equal the original cash outlay. A maximum permissable pay-back period is determined in the first place: 1, 2, 3, 4 or 5 years are frequently used.

TABLE XIV: PAY-BACK PERIOD ANALYSIS OF INVESTMENT

Investment	A	B	C	D	E	F
Pay-back period	1	2	$2\frac{1}{3}$	1	2	$1\frac{1}{4}$
Ranking	1=	4=	6	1=	4=	3

Table XIV shows the ranking of the various investments using the pay-back period method. Because the calculations fail to consider cash proceeds earned after the pay-back date, we find A and D are ranked equally. A second weakness of the method is that it fails to take account of differences in the timing of the proceeds earned prior to the pay-back date. B and E are also ranked equally, but E would be a better investment on this score.

Average Annual Proceeds

This method calculates for each investment the average annual proceeds per £ of outlay. To illustrate, if we take investment C, the total return is £18,000. The proceeds per £ outlay (the original £10,000) is therefore £1.80.

TABLE XV: AVERAGE ANNUAL PROCEEDS
ANALYSIS OF INVESTMENT

Investment	A	B	C	D	E	F
Average annual proceeds per £	1.0	0.5	0.6	0.53	0.5	0.6
Ranking	1	5=	2=	4	5=	2=

Since the return on the investment is over three years, the average annual proceeds per £ of outlay is £0.60.

It can be seen from Table XV that the ranking so achieved from this method provides a heavy bias towards short-lived investments with high cash yields. It is for this reason that investment choice A ranks alone in first place. No account is taken of the timing of payments, yet there is little doubt that £1 today is worth more than £1 in a year's time. A further weakness is that the weights of the proceeds have no effect. An investment of £10,000 which yielded £10,000 in year one only would rank equally with an alternative investment of £10,000 which yielded £10,000 in each of the succeeding ten years. The latter investment is obviously better than the former, but this method of analysis would not identify it to be so.

Discounted Cash Flow Methods

The principle of Discounted Cash Flow (often written DCF) is that future returns on an investment are discounted back to any equivalent value, or worth, at the present time. In other words, if a sum of money were available at some time in the future, how much money would one be prepared to accept now as a substitute for that future sum? The money which would replace that future sum is known as its Present Value.

As an example consider the Present Value of £100 payable in two years. This is the amount of money necessary to be invested now which will grow to £100 in two years time. We can answer the question explicitly only if we know the rate of interest and the frequency at which it is compounded. We shall assume the latter to be compounded annually.

£100 invested today at 3% grows to £103 at the end of year one and to £106.09 at the end of year two. The Present Value of £106.09 at the end of two years is therefore £100. However, we are normally more interested in the Present Value of £100 available at the end of two years, say, and this works out to be £100 divided by 1.0609, which is equal to £94.26. We can therefore say that £94.26 invested now at 3% compound interest will grow to £100 at the end of two years.

In the example above we have assumed the rate of interest to be 3%. At the present time, this is a particularly low rate; to be more general, let us take the rate of interest as r%. Using investment E from Table XIII as an example, we should like to find the Present Values of £6,000 in year one, £4,000 in year two and £5,000 in year three. Let x_1, x_2 and x_3 be the respective Present Values. Then, from our previous discussion, it can be seen that:

$$x_1 = \text{£6,000 divided by } (1 + \tfrac{r}{100})$$
$$x_2 = \text{£4,000 divided by } (1 + \tfrac{r}{100})^2$$
$$x_3 = \text{£5,000 divided by } (1 + \tfrac{r}{100})^3$$

and the total Present Value of the proceeds of investment E is therefore x_1 plus x_2 plus x_3. Given an interest rate r, we can determine precisely what this Present Value is.

It is apparent that any series of cash proceeds can be converted to an equivalent Present Value. The required calculations may at first sight look daunting, but this may be overcome by the use of tables. A selection from such tables is shown in Table XVI.

DCF methods provide, then, a method of taking account of the timings during the full life of a project. It will be noted that any series of proceeds can be made to have the same Present Value simply by choosing appropriate values for each rate of interest, r.

Net Present Value

Net Present Value is defined as Present Value of proceeds minus Present Value of outlays. In the examples of Table XIII, Present Value of outlay is always the value of the outlay itself. Investment decisions will be required, however, when outlays occur not only at the beginning of a project, but also in later years. The purchase of

TABLE XVI: DISCOUNTED CASH FLOW
ANALYSIS OF INVESTMENT

Number of years n	Compound amount factor @ 5 per cent	Present Value factor @ 5 per cent
1	1.050	0.9524
2	1.103	0.9070
3	1.158	0.8638
4	1.216	0.8227
5	1.276	0.7835
6	1.340	0.7462
7	1.407	0.7107
8	1.478	0.6768
9	1.551	0.6446
10	1.629	0.6139
15	2.079	0.4810
20	2.653	0.3769
25	3.386	0.2953
30	4.322	0.2314
35	5.516	0.1813
40	7.040	0.1421
45	8.985	0.1113
50	11.467	0.0872

machinery and its subsequent maintenance would be an example. Just as proceeds of an investment have Present Values, so do outlays. These may be discounted back in exactly the same ways as proceeds, to provide Present Value of all outlays for a project.

It is necessary to choose an appropriate rate of interest in order to be able to calculate Net Present Value of an investment and its proceeds. In the examples of Table XIII, let us assume 30%, in which case the ranking of the investments becomes as shown in Table XVII.

TABLE XVII: NET PRESENT VALUE ANALYSIS OF INVESTMENT

Investment	A	B	C	D	E	F
Ranking	6	5	3	2	4	1

Yield

The yield of an investment is that rate of interest which will make the Present Value of the proceeds equal to the Present Value of the outlays. In effect, this means the rate of interest which will provide a Net Present Value of zero. Put another way, if it had been necessary to borrow the money to pay for the outlay in the first place, the rate of interest which provides a Net Present Value of zero (i.e. the yield) is the highest rate of interest the borrower could afford to pay in order to break even on the investment.

If we look again at the investment choices of Table XIII, we find, as we would expect, that the yield for each investment is different. Table XVIII shows the yield values, and the corresponding rankings. Referring again to investment choice E, the procedure to calculate yield is to find a value of r which makes x_1 plus x_2 plus x_3 equal to £10,000. This is a particularly difficult calculation, but is helped by the provision of tables, as discussed previously. The yield percentage would be determined by substituting values for r until the N.P.V. were made equal to zero.

TABLE XVIII: YIELD VALUES OF INVESTMENTS

Investment	A	B	C	D	E	F
Yield %	0	23	27	37	24	44
Rank	6	5	3	2	4	1

SHORTCOMINGS AND RESERVATIONS

Particularly in times of inflation it is not always possible to say far in advance what the return on a particular investment will be over the years. Even without the effect of inflation, there is no way in which the business man can be sure that his investment will turn out to be as successful as he would hope. Not only might the annual returns be different from those which he expects, but he may have to commit additional financial outlays, such as replacement costs for worn-out machinery, for which he did not plan.

In assessing various investment strategies, it is not necessary to decide in advance upon a rate of interest which will apply throughout the life of the investment. In reality, interest rates change year by year. Although theoretically possible, to take changing rates into account would be arithmetically complex and, futhermore, there is no way of knowing what they will be before they actually occur.

Making a choice between investments depends a great deal upon unknown future data. This is not unlike many other kinds of decision which must be taken, but it does make it that much more hazardous. The most important factor, however, is that if a choice must be made between investment strategies, each must be brought to a common denomination and each treated in a consistent, logical, and rational way.

DISCUSSION QUESTIONS

1. What are the most commonly used methods of assessing the viability of an investment?

2. What are their disadvantages?

3. In what way does the DCF method overcome these disadvantages?

4. Nevertheless, what are the disadvantages of DCF?

5. Explain the difference between Net Present Value and yield.

6. Applying Table XVI to investment D in Table XIII, show that the Net Present Value with a 5% interest factor is £4,836.40.

CHAPTER XV

What, then, is O.R.?

In the preceding fourteen chapters of this book we have discussed various mathematical techniques for solving management problems. These techniques have over the years achieved considerable success and have played an important part in improving the efficiency and hence profitability of the many companies which have employed them. Yet even with that record of success, we must register words of caution.

Just as it would be wrong for the plumber to use the tools of his trade, the spanner and the blow-torch, to carry out the tasks of the electrician, so it is dangerous for O.R. techniques to be applied in the wrong context. Not every queueing problem can be solved by Queueing Theory. Only with a linear objective function and linear constraints can a problem be solved by Linear Programming. Unfortunately, the enthusiastic and inexperienced O.R. scientist may be tempted to make his problem fit a technique, rather than find the right technique for the problem. As a result, a non-existent problem may be solved that keeps the O.R. practitioner busy but does little for the company.

Because certain mathematical techniques exist, it does not follow that these are the only ones which must be used. Often O.R. methodology is applied to problems using the thinking of O.R. to develop new kinds of solutions. One in particular which we have not discussed as a topic so far is that known as "heuristics". In simple language, it is an attempt to copy existing ways of tackling problems (for example, understanding the thinking process of the production scheduler when he makes out his production schedule) and uses trial and error methods. The solution is usually achieved with the use of a computer, which carries out a systematic procedure.

A great deal of recent O.R. thinking has centred upon qualitative aspects of business as well as the quantitative. This strays into the area of the behavioural scientist. The objectives of companies have been studied in some depth and we are now beginning to think not only in terms of financial return but also in terms of worker satisfaction and of energy accounting, i.e. how much fossil energy can be saved by following each possible decision course.

To say what O.R. is, is to bring us back to the discussion in Chapter I and the realisation that the O.R. Society itself is seeking to redefine O.R. If we say that it is a scientific approach to solving business and management problems, using the methodology of science as broadly as possible, then we shall have defined O.R. for all practical purposes as closely as we need. The high standing of O.R. today with its record of success speaks for itself.

Index

120 INDEX